Mr. Integrity: 21 Months with a Catholic Con Man

By

Wendy Quirk

This book is a work of fiction. Places, events, and situations in this story are purely fictional. Any resemblance to actual persons, living or dead, is coincidental.

ISBN: 1-4033-8311-1 (e-book)
ISBN: 1-4033-8312-X (Paperback)

This book is printed on acid free paper.

1stBooks - rev. 10/15/02

Acknowledgement

In appreciation for the incredible blessings, lessons, and inspirations that have been given me, I give thanks to God for always showing me the way, and for my father, whose spirit lives all around us. Special thanks to my two incredibly perfect children, my ever-loving mom, my sister (the amazing healer), my wonderful brother, and all their families for being with me every step of the way. Many thanks to the incredible and inspiring Reverend Brian Anderson of the First Church of Religious Science in Vista, Ca. A huge debt of gratitude is owed to all

iii

my friends for standing by my side during the darkness, and pulling me back into the light again. A heartfelt thanks of gratitude and appreciation to all the readers who bought this book.

Dedication

Dedicated to Michael

"*The tragedy of life is what dies in the hearts and souls of people while they live.*"   *Albert Einstein*

Table of Contents

Chapter One: Watch Out

Most of us know about the various types of scams and cons that are lurking out there, just waiting for some unsuspecting, honest, trusting person to get sucked in. They are everywhere, from the oddly-dressed airport pan-handlers pretending to collect money for needy people, to the "internet opportunity-of-a-lifetime" scams that bombard us with emails us every other hour. I personally have had several scam-related experiences besides "Mr. Integrity" that I will share with you. I feel that is important to make people aware of things and situations that they may not otherwise think about, and I have had a few interesting ones.

Firstly, be especially aware of hotel seminars offering a highly-hyped business opportunity that involves setting you up with a 4-year lease from a Massachusetts company for overpriced, e-commerce enabled web site equipment. They want you to sign a 4-year lease right then and there. The only way out of the lease is to cancel it by fax within 48 hours. Well, anyone knows that when you sign something like that, you have every intention of using it, thinking you are dealing with reputable firms. Why would you cancel something 48 hours later that you intended to use for your business? Based on my personal experience with this situation, it was possibly fraudulent from the beginning. I was sold an internet web site package, and ended up with the lease for $69/month for the e-commerce part of the web site. My business was to consist of a web site offering new age health and healing products and information. I worked for months putting this business together, and finally submitted it to the company that was supposed to build the web site. After waiting the allowed time for them to build my web site, they mysteriously disappeared without a

3

trace, leaving me with the lease for the equipment. While waiting for the never-developed web site, I lost all of my new and cutting edge products to other vendors, and ended up in a very costly 4-year lease that I had been paying for since the day I signed the papers. (I assumed that when I started selling the products, I would recover that money I already spent, and have a profitable internet business.) After learning of the disappearance of the web package company, I stopped paying on the lease and continue to be billed for it. From information I obtained on the internet, this leasing company charges more than normal amounts for e-commerce equipment, and apparently has so many complaints that the state of Massachusetts is investigating them.

Also, please watch out for young people that come to your door selling magazines for a Irvine, CA based company. I have ordered magazines twice from this company, and have problems both times with never receiving magazines. When I asked for a refund, they refused. Then they offered to send me the magazines, but said it would take another 4 months. That was 9 months after I paid for them! Sadly, companies like this are everywhere, just waiting to take our money, yet unwilling to operate with scruples and integrity. I particularly don't like this one because I think they use unsuspecting children to get the public's money, then keep the money for up to 4 months before sending magazines. In my case, they claim they lost the order, and it just didn't get put into the computer. That seems odd, since I gave the young man at the door a check, then sent the second installment a week or so later. Two separate checks they cashed, and the company still made the same mistake—twice? *Hmmm*.

There are people everywhere who have no qualms about unscrupulously obtaining money from others, so it is imperative to always be careful, know what you are investing in, read the fine print, and always read contracts and agreements carefully. Complications can arise that you would *never* expect!

Here's an example of another situation I experienced. This one pertains to an apartment rental lease. My daughter lived in the college town of Greeley, Colorado several years ago, and wanted to live off campus. She was shown a rental property by a supposedly reputable and established management company. She was immediately asked to sign a lease for that property, being told that there were waiting lists for rentals. She later had to decline the apartment because she found out she was under contract with the university dormitory housing department. I had originally signed the papers for the university housing contract, and my daughter was unaware of the contractual agreement. I think that could be the case for many college students, since the parents are usually financially responsible, and make all of the financial arrangements with colleges. My daughter was billed for the so-called "lost rental revenue" by the management company. In my opinion, a rental agency claiming to be in business for 17 years in a college town probably should have known that college students living in the dorms are under a housing contract. I wonder if there are other students who signed apartment leases thinking it was OK to move off campus, only to be billed by unscrupulous apartment rental companies for "lost rent revenue." Fortunately my daughter's lease had a clause stating "no rent was due if possession of the property was not delivered," so she is not legally responsible. Who would have thought of a situation like that arising? I am sure they are everywhere, and we need to be alert and aware. We live in a very money oriented world, and being a decent, trusting, law abiding citizen doesn't always mean that we can assume other people operate the same way.

Consumers must also be particularly careful in this digital/electronic lifestyle to which we are rapidly becoming accustomed, especially here in the United States. There is an abundance of information available regarding the various types of fraud and scams that go on here, as well as worldwide. There are internet sites that discuss internet sites that fraud people! I have seen books, articles, and a multitude of other resources one can utilize if they are considering a business opportunity, researching suspected fraud, or just gathering information. Telephone fraud runs rampant in the United States. People pose as agents trying to collect money for so-called reputable organizations, or many other highly creative ways to cheat the public (especially the elderly) by getting pledge money or credit card numbers over the phone.

Did you know, for example, that if you dial area code 809 (located in the Dominican Republic) it could cost $2,425 per minute? The 809 area code is similar to 900 numbers in the USA. Since 809 is not in the US, it's not monitored by the U.S. regulations of 900 numbers notifying the caller of rates and charges. (You could receive a call from a scammer urging you to call a number beginning with area code 809 to claim a prize, or other bogus reasons.)

Another very popular type of phone fraud consists of someone posing to be a phone repair person conducting a test of the phone lines. They ask the victim to push 9, 0, and the pound sign (#), and then hang up. Unbeknownst to the consumer, pushing 90# actually gives the criminal on the other end of the line full access to your telephone line, enabling them to place long distance calls and bill them to your phone number. These types of fraud are proliferating exponentially in direct parallel with our expanding, electronic, online universe.

The other side of the double-edged, electronic sword of fraud is the availability of personal information on just about anybody. For a meager amount of money, anyone can track down their former lover, friend, enemy, relative, or a business associate. Using the tools now available online, many family members, lost loves, adopted children, and old friends have reconnected with someone they thought might be "lost" forever. One might also use these tools to investigate a potential love interest, or relationship partner. This information could prove to be invaluable for someone who is already involved in, or planning to be in a serious relationship. Solid reassurance that Mr. or Miss right isn't really Mr. or Miss con artist/criminal is a justifiable action for many people. Granted, that might seem a bit cold and callused to be "spying" on someone that you are supposed to be emotionally involved with, but let's face it—not everyone out there has the same values, morals, and beliefs that others may possess. (In my case, that meager amount of money it costs to investigate someone would have been worth it's weight in 1998 dot.com stock, had I known what I'm about to

reveal in this book!)

> *From the beginning of time, man has been untruthful to others for personal gain. When we trust our instincts and listen to our internal feelings, only then can we tap into the real truth that is always within us.*

Chapter Two: "Love Bandits"

Since my particular experience being conned involved a man, I may be referring to the term "con man" or "he" intermittently through the book. I certainly recognize that many men and women equally have been in my situation, and it could happen to anyone of any age, race, or sex. Referencing the male gender is strictly for the sole purpose of consistency in telling the story and not a subtle attempt at male bashing—I promise!

I will now begin sharing with you my personal experience involving another type of deception and fraud;

one that is more subtle, and becomes multi-dimensional in how it can affect your life. It is not just about money, papers, signatures, contracts, agreements, credit cards, or any other type of deceptive transaction strictly involving money. Granted, those types of fraud can be extremely devastating in that financial segment of our lives, but they usually only involve one dimension of the whole human experience.

The perpetrators of this other type of deception are commonly referred to as "Love Bandits"—members of the opposite sex masqueraded as a love interest, that play with your heart and emotions as well as your pocketbook. Their sole purpose in initiating a relationship with you revolves around extracting money or valuables from you in various different ways. They make a sport out of using and manipulating your emotional feelings for personal gain unconstrained by morality, and without any conscious thought of responsibility. They use you for everything possible and make you think you owe it to them.

As long as you are financially well off, they continue their deception and bravely live a life of charades, pretending to care about you. After they destroy you financially and the money is gone (or the credit cards maxed out, as in my case), they seek out and spot their next target, abruptly move on, blame you for the relationship not working, and leave a trail of personal and financial destruction behind them. "Crimes of Persuasion" they call it, and a really good con artist can be extremely persuasive. These types of people are usually all lies, and no substance. Typically, they are completely incapable of accepting responsibility for anything in their life. Shallow would be an excellent term for categorizing this personality type. In their life and relationships, they are living on the outer circumference of their own soul, focusing only on the material world. Their life and their existence is for outward materialistic gain only, with no compassion whatsoever for whoever gets hurt along the way. Their quasi-trustworthy persona paves the way for fraudulent opportunities in their relentless pursuit of financial gain. They know how to extract the exact response from someone they need, and manipulate the opposite sex from strictly an emotional standpoint, using the person's vulnerability as a way to get what they want.

Much of that manipulation is guilt-based. If they can make you feel guilty, they create an opening to drive in a wedge of deceit that will most assuredly destroy your life. They are usually pathological liars, and a master at quick answers. Sharply but subtly they defer the questions you ask them, and parlay their response into something that sounds logical to you at the time. In actuality, I think that "Love Bandit" con artists are worse than a common thief who breaks into a home or business and steals your possessions. At least a thief gets right to the objective, takes what he wants, and doesn't trample on your emotions in the process.

A good "Love Bandit" likes to move fast into a relationship; for one thing, they fear that if the relationship moves too slowly, they may be more vulnerable to being exposed. The faster they get their hooks into your home, belongings, and finances, the easier it is for them to take what they want and get out quickly. By moving at a fast pace, the lies and manipulation tend to be more believable because you don't have time to analyze what is happening in the relationship. As humans, we tend to be much more gullible and vulnerable at the beginning of a relationship when everything is new, and the excitement of the romance clouds our judgement.

The "Love Bandit" will promise a long term commitment early in the relationship and pretend to be serious with you, to soften any possible mixed signals that may be trying to creep into your mind. They coerce you into believing that the relationship must move to the next level quickly, thus molding and shaping the perimeters of the relationship to suit their needs and master plan, with them in full control. Amazingly, this type of person has you thoroughly convinced that you are the one in control and the one setting the pace. What isn't seen by the person being used and cheated, is the big picture that the "Love Bandit" already has planned out. Most normal people think they are in any relationship for building a personal, romantic connection with someone, when actually they are being set up to become the pieces of destruction left behind the path of the "Love Bandit."

In this type of situation, the con artist sees his target, implements his plan, and enters into a relationship as he would a business. He usually has a specific goal or target, and designs a carefully laid plan of attack. Meanwhile, the other person is seeing the con artist only as a love interest, and can be easily manipulated when in a state of emotional highs, or emotional vulnerability.

The writing of this story was a culmination of some very strong motives for me. First, despite the mental anguish of strolling down memory lane and dredging up the unpleasant mental pictures of the turmoil, pain and suffering my last relationship caused me, I feel that telling this story might prevent others from falling into the traps of other similar, twisted-minded people. I want to share my experiences in hopes that it will save someone else from the agony I endured as a result of a deceitful relationship. Perhaps you or someone you know has doubts as to the character and integrity of their lover or friend. I'm hoping that someone reading this information might be able to step out of their own relationship long enough to take a closer look at anything that doesn't feel right. If sharing my experiences in this book helps anyone else see a red-flag, question their own reasons for getting into or staying in a bad relationship, or experience even a small revelation, I would be thrilled.

Furthermore, this person that I was involved with is still out there, currently working on my successor—a nice, unsuspecting woman from a wealthy background. He seems to have a history of short, and sometimes tumultuous relationships, and I think he will most likely be on the prowl again soon. If even one person avoids this man because of my book, it will all have been worthwhile. I believe God puts people into our lives for a very specific purpose, and for lessons that we need to learn while we are in this dimension called life on earth. Lessons are valuable for our own personal growth and development. If someone else can benefit from my lessons, then it is no accident that they are reading this.

Additionally, I am not the only person who trusted the individual who destroyed me financially. There are others as well who got swindled by being involved with this person, and it is my commitment is to do everything possible to get them paid back. Publishing this bizarre story was the only idea I could come up with to try and generate money to get all of the video project creditors repaid, including me. The customers who unknowingly purchased the un-produced videos at the *2001 Laughlin River Run* will also be on the list of creditors.

This could be called a last ditch-effort (and probably a long shot!) to salvage my credit, my credibility, and my name, and repay everyone else. To my knowledge, the unpaid debts from this project could be as high as $100,000. Personally suffering from a severe case of "post-traumatic credit card debt syndrome," writing this book seemed like my only possible salvation to try and generate the lost revenue for all of us.

If you purchased this book, I can't thank you enough. Many people were hurt by this con artist, and it is my commitment to do whatever it takes to get the creditors repaid. Aside from me, there is at least one other person who is owed a considerable sum, a string of smaller creditors, several major motorcycle businesses, and the event customers who got swindled as well. They have all given up hope of ever seeing a dime of the money they entrusted to this particular con artist.

I might be praying for a miracle here, but I believe in miracles, and one never knows what God has in store for us. When we are committed to helping others, amazing miracles can happen. So, on a wing and a prayer, here's hoping for something amazing and miraculous.

Be alert, be aware, and be careful in giving away your trust. Real trust must be earned through honesty, character, and integrity. Go slowly, do some research, and really know someone well before becoming financially involved with them.

Chapter Three: The Beginning

"He's forty," my friend announced. Her response to my question about his age was delayed by a momentary hesitation, but I was so taken aback by the nature of the phone call in general that I didn't catch what would later prove to be the very first lie of the deceitful relationship destined to unfold. (He was actually 39 and wouldn't celebrate his 40th birthday until 11 months later.)

It all started when I had gone out with a friend the evening prior to the phone call—St. Patrick's Day, 1999. As my friend Laura and I sat at the round, outdoor concrete fire pit, chatting away, our attention was focused on a particularly nice looking guy Laura was interested in meeting. Until I stood up to move my chair so she could have a better view, I failed to notice that another close female friend of mine was sitting directly behind me. Upon recognizing her, we both stood up and exchanged the usual chic to chic hugs, "Hi's," and "how are you doing's." She was sitting with a man I didn't recognize as her current significant other I had met, so I assumed that she was now with someone else and had moved on. We conversed for a while, then invited her and her

32

male companion to join us. Not wanting to bring up the subject who she was with and why, I steered the conversation away from her and the attractive male she was with. The dynamics of the conversation between the two of them was interesting if not a bit unusual, but it wasn't until some time later that she made reference to him as her brother, Michael. That explains it! Instantly relieved that she was still in her real relationship and not dating someone new, I felt a bit more relaxed and comfortable. I then vaguely remembered some prior mention of her having a brother in the spa cover business. "Hmmm, so this was him! Cute, funny, and probably has a girlfriend," were my only thoughts on the guy. I was not out looking for men, and really had no interest in starting up anything with anyone. I evidently missed the signals Michael was sending me, but he never directly expressed any interest in me at all that evening, so I didn't give it another thought. Laura, however, managed to reel in her catch, and he soon joined us. The five of us talked for about an hour or so, then exchanged good-byes. We had previously talked about going out dancing on the following Saturday, and as a courtesy, invited Michael and Laura's new love interest to join us. It seemed like a fun idea, but I didn't really expect Michael to show up and had no particular attachment to it whatsoever.

The next day the phone rang and I was surprised when Michael's sister said, "My brother wants to go out with you." I am not one of those women who attract a lot of men into my life, nor do I always need, or want to be in a relationship with a man. I was definitely not out looking for a man in my life that fateful night! I have been single for a while and my primary focus has been on career objectives, and not relationships. I read a lot (mostly metaphysical and self-help books) and love watching movies, so I stay busy when I'm home. However, the men that do wander into my life (or come crashing in, as the case may be) are, for whatever the reason, usually somewhat younger than I am. As I learned from prior experience, being in a relationship with someone younger does pose it's challenges, and makes me a bit skittish.

Although the thought of seeing Michael again was not entirely unappealing, I just wasn't sure it would be a good idea. (He looked like a guy who would be somewhere in his mid-thirties, and in my mind that spelled disaster from a relationship point of view.) Currently hovering in the "over fifty" category, I was strongly leaning toward a resounding "no" answer. Had his sister's reply about his age started with the word thirty *anything*, it would have been a definite "no" on my part. (For me, the words dating someone and thirty anything just shouldn't be together in the same sentence!) Dating someone more than 10-15 years younger can possibly be something that would work out, but it has been my experience that the larger the age difference, the more difficult it is for a relationship to run smoothly. I'm not closed off completely to the idea, but usually approach it cautiously.

Apparently, I wasn't cautious enough when it came to this man!

Reluctantly, I agreed to meet Michael at one of the local dance bars that coming Saturday night. (I don't remember anything else about my conversation with his sister that day, but I did learn later from Michael that he was at his sister's house when she called me, and he heard the entire conversation.) That Saturday night, Laura and I wandered into the club and saw Michael at a table near the front door, close to the band. He was wearing one of those neat, peasant-style shirts that has gathering at the shoulders and full sleeves, with the Mandarin-type collar. The white shirt next to his tanned face made for a striking, and roguishly handsome image. With his dark hair and brown eyes added into the equation, the overall package scored a ten in my book. It was total sensory overload! We danced, laughed, and had a terrific time. He has a true gift of being witty and funny, which was a nice, added feature to the usual first-date uneasiness and ice-breaking process. We were talking about vacations and various other topics when the word paradise came up in the conversation. "What's your idea of paradise?" I asked Michael, over the music. He quickly quipped,

Wendy Quirk

"A weekend with you." Lord help me, I thought! The man was charming!

From there, our relationship progressed (regressed would *now* be the appropriate word) to movies, a Padre Game, lunch meetings, and dinners. We continued to go out steadily on into the summer months, and I found him charming and irresistible. Every day, he would compliment me on my appearance, my hair, or my intelligence. He claims he likes women who have a good command of the English language, and apparently he thought I was in that category. When we went out, he would tell me how lucky he was to be with the most attractive woman in the restaurant. Wow! Spoken like a true boyfriend! His nickname for me was "doll" or "dollface" and I thought it was cute and fun. I am basically a very trusting person, and this made it very difficult to have any doubts about a man who always had something nice to say about me. I stupidly thought that the man had been attracted to me, and didn't realize I had entered stage one as the target of his con game. He planned exactly what to say because he needed to create and maintain an element of trust early in the relationship as part of his con efforts. Even though the flattery may have been a bit excessive, I had no reason to doubt

41

his sincerity. I never made the connection that all the flattery I was given during the course of the relationship was simply a tool of the trade to sink the hooks in more quickly, and keep them there until he completed his game.

> *Be aware of insincerity masqueraded as flattery. It will take you exactly where the con artist wants you to go—-into a state of complete trust.*

Chapter Four: Infiltration

Michael claimed he had previously owned a condo in Carlsbad, but said he sold it and moved in with his parents. I was never told why he sold the condo or where the money went. He didn't seem to have much money when we met, so I thought maybe he sold it to get out of the payments. (One of my information sources later indicated that he actually rented the place and never owned it.) I later met some of his neighbors at a dinner party so I assume he did live there. Nevertheless, his parents were "unexpectedly" moving to Temecula, California (about an hour from us

43

here in Carlsbad) and wanted him to get his own place. Jokingly, Michael said "they left me a note on the door." According to Michael, it was all very sudden and he really was out a place to live. I have no way of knowing whether or not there was any truth to that, or if it was just a convenient opening to slide his way into my place. Based on results, I'm guessing the latter.

"Of course you can stay here until you have a plan" was the only response I would have been capable of giving at that time. We had been dating for about two or three months, and I assumed that it would be temporary, and that he would start looking for his own place. I have always been one to open my doors to anyone who was in need of a short-term place to stay. (Some of my kids' teenage friends were among that list.) At the time, I had no idea the situation living with Michael would be long term, or the effects so devastating.

He gradually infiltrated his belongings into my apartment, but traveled lightly for the most part. Clothing, a few personal effects, some small mementos and pictures, a child's car seat, and a photo of him in the Marine Corps was just about the sum total of what came here. I didn't get a real clear picture of his life in the Marine Corps, but the perception that I formulated, based on his discussion about it, was one of a less than perfect experience during his term of enlistment, and possibly a less than honorable discharge. He had a few more personal effects in storage, but apparently just walked away from his last two relationships leaving most of the household items behind, or so he claimed.

As our relationship cruised along, bits and pieces of his history began to be revealed. I didn't pry into his personal life, and he respected that aspect of our relationship. I do not believe that a relationship means ownership of another, and I respect that a partner needs their space. Everyone has their own secrets that may or may not ever be disclosed. Most of the information I am relaying in this book was voluntarily revealed by Michael during our time together, without my digging.

Michael was in the spa business, and was manufacturing an inexpensive spa cover lift that he openly admitted was a knock-off of the original, more popular one on the market. He copied the pattern and design of his competitor's product, and hired several companies to manufacture the different parts. Then he hired the Developmentally Disabled in San Diego to assemble and ship the product out.

He told me that he had been married twice before, and had 2 sons. His older son was by his first wife, and there were apparently no additional kids with Michael by the second wife. I met the older son, and immediately took a liking to him. He was around 18 at that time, and lived in Northern California. I got to spend time with the older son on several different occasions, and established a strong connection with him in a very short time. We wrote letters back and forth, and spoke on the phone occasionally.

His second wife had children from a previous marriage, and Michael seemed proud of how he helped support them and contributed financially in getting them through college. He indicated that his second wife was Italian, and really loved him a lot. "She begged me not to leave, even followed me to the airport," was his rendition of the ending for yet another failed marriage. I am seeing now a different picture about what really happened in that marriage. Since our parting, I learned that Michael still owed her thousands of dollars he borrowed against her family's property. His reason told to me for leaving her was wishy-washy, and inconsistent. There was something about her being too co-dependent, and not motivated. At the time I had this picture in my mind of a fiery, hot-blooded Italian woman, running after Michael in the airport, begging him to stay. Now, my mind creates a similar scenario, with one added feature—she's screaming after him carrying a baseball bat!

The younger son Michael spoke about was from a relationship with a woman who he evidently met after his second divorce, and cared for very much. Why they split up is not clear, but according to him she got too clingy and possessive. (You'd think he could come up with something different!) According to my other sources, he was supposedly stalking her after the relationship fizzled out. I have to now wonder what her side of the story would disclose.

Still snowed by the charm, I had no cause to discredit his explanation at the time. I really didn't care one way or the other, feeling like it was not by business. Apparently, she wanted children and got pregnant unexpectedly by Michael. Michael said that he loved their baby son very much and spent hours playing and reading with him. He would pick the son up at day care and spend time with him. Evidently, things between them began to change, and he claims that he ended the relationship with her. He did confess that he owed her back child support money. His work background included the trucking business when he was with her, and had a much larger income during that time. Apparently, he hauled U.S. Mail in Chicago, and did very well financially. According to him, he was supposed to pay his youngest son's mother $1500 per month child support, based on the trucking business income. I recently was told that he walked away from that trucking business, leaving the trucks on the side of the road, and the employees unpaid. (That behavior paradigm will repeat itself later in the story.)

The spa business generated considerably less income for Michael, so paying that much child support with a severe reduction in income was not possible. His ex-girlfriend finally cut off his visitation rights and initiated court proceedings for payment. According to Michael, sometime later, she repossessed his jeep and only form of transportation, while he was at the day care facility, picking up his son. (As I recall, this was sometime during the summer of 1999.) I went out to breakfast with Michael one day and he had his youngest son with him, so at least the part about the child's existence was true. I do believe one thing—that at the time, Michael did care for this child...at the time anyway.

Michael took a job as a cook at the Grand Deli in Carlsbad just so he could show the courts that he was working at a very low income job. Hoping that he could manipulate the judicial system the way he does relationship partners, he tried to prove to the courts how much his income has dropped, and how his lifestyle has changed. This plan was short-lived when he had difficulty working with the Hispanic employees at the deli, so he finally quit. After our parting, I found a work check stub he left behind from the

Grand Deli. Through information available on the internet, I learned that the Social Security number he gave to the deli didn't match what was probably his real Social Security number.

Michael retained a lawyer to regain visitation rights, but it got very expensive and he finally dropped the matter entirely. In order to continue, it was mandatory that Michael go to the state appointed doctor for psychological evaluation as a routing part of determining custody issues. That would have involved several thousand dollars in fees to the court appointed psychologist.

In retrospect, I think he feared that his manipulative and dishonest way of life would have been revealed during this evaluation. At the time, I was actually quite surprised to learn that he was dropping the case. I personally can't imagine not being able to see my children. For him, I am guessing that it just wasn't important enough to risk taking the psychological evaluation, and to generate the extra money for the evaluation and legal fees.

Months later and well into the relationship, I was shocked to learn that he also had a daughter by his first wife. When I questioned why he had never mentioned her before, he adamantly persisted that he did mention her, and that I had been mistaken. I thought it was odd at the time, but I felt it was none of my business to pry, so I dismissed it, doubting myself and thinking maybe he was right. Now, I can only wonder what mystery surrounds the relationship (or lack of) with his daughter. Why he would maintain a relationship with his older son and younger son, but not his daughter? Why would he deny her existence to me by saying he had 2 children and not 3? What kind of person lies about how many children they have?

It is crucial to question the values of people who place more importance on money than on their own children. If they can't respect their own children, they won't respect you either.

Chapter Five: Back in the

Harley Seat

Michael rather suddenly decided to sell the spa cover lift business. Apparently, some of his customers were being questioned about the cover lift product by the original manufacturer who had the patent. He sold his business for around $20,000, as I recall. He got around $15,000 up front, and with it bought a very nice 1996 Harley. Claiming that the Harley he previously used was owned and repossessed by his step-daughter from the second marriage, he was thrilled to have one back in his life again. He stated that he legally signed over his previous Harley to the step-daughter's name, but he legally owned it—"just a business transaction, of course." I thought nothing of it at the time, not knowing anything about his business dealings with his second wife and her children.

Michael asked me if I would put the recently acquired Harley in my name until his court case with his ex-girlfriend was over. I didn't see any harm in that, and figured it would only be for a short time. Since I would be the legal owner, I couldn't think of any reason to not help him out. I didn't feel at the time that it would pose any threat or problem, because it was paid for. As you can probably guess, that gesture caused some considerable problems and interesting events on down the line.

One of his favorite expressions was "business is business" and he used it whenever he needed or tried to justify any of his actions regarding money. (I used to think that he was a very brilliant businessman, because he could generate money quickly, and sell anything to anyone.) Truthfully, I think he uses that phrase to really mean "since this is business and not personal, it's OK to screw you out of money, but don't take it personally!" I now know that the word "business" to Michael means hide your assets, never pay taxes, never sign your name to anything so you can't be held responsible, and cheat anyone you can out of money. He much later disclosed to me that he hasn't paid taxes to the IRS in many years.

At any rate, having a Harley again was a huge boost for his ego. He is a man who seemed to be very much impressed by looks and outward appearances, so the prestige of being a Harley owner and rider allowed him an opportunity to segeway into that elite, social group of riders called HOG's. He was constantly polishing and shining his new toy, while intermittently adding the typical ornate, chromed accessories to further enhance the image and look of the bike. Michael usually wore black clothing and silver-framed sunglasses, and knew he looked good on his prized possession. He "accessorized" himself as well as the bike, buying the vests, pins, jackets, emblems, and headbands necessary to create that "I'm a Harley rider" image seemingly so important to him. He never left the apartment without asking me, "How do I look?" At the time, I saw him as the embodiment of pure sex appeal—Wow! "And he was *my* guy!" I thought proudly.

The local Harley Owner's Group met one evening every week at the outdoor bar of the Coyote Bar and Grill in Carlsbad. Michael attended those meetings quite frequently, utilizing every possible opportunity to socialize with the other Harley riders. He loves to tell jokes and comedy skits heavily laden with sexual innuendoes. This particular environment provided the perfect setting and perfect audience, allowing him to be the center of attention. Using his wit and humor, he could readily grab onto any available amount of hero worship or acceptance from his biker peers. He made a wide circle of acquaintances through this avenue, and I'm sure that they all received the gift of laughter he seemed so desperate to give people to gain attention. (By the end of this book, you will know why many of those people now have a different opinion of the man who once made them laugh.) He spent many of his weekend hours attending the organized Harley rides and events. He made friends easily with his outgoing and witty personality, and through this avenue, later set up a network of volunteers and employees for the business that would come to be known as Flagship Productions/Flagship Entertainment.

During this time, Michael did intermittent work for some friends in the spa business after he sold his cover lift business. This provided him with a small amount of cash flow until the new business was formulated. He delivered and repaired spas for a local spa manufacturing company. It was physically grueling, but he liked the social interaction with the customers, and it offered him another avenue for being the center of attention and telling jokes. He appeared to always be seeking some type of attention, approval, or validation from others, but was also very confident about other things. He understands business concepts and is a whiz at instantaneously calculating numbers in his head. I would guess that most good con artists have that innate ability to calculate things quickly. Tool of the trade, maybe?

Certainly an intriguing person, he was also very complex at the same time. His adroit, cunning, quick-thinking mind made him an expert at having an immediate response to almost any question or comment made. Michael liked to always appear smart—if he didn't agree or approve of something said, he would go to almost any lengths to convince you that it was always the other person who was incompetent or stupid. He was so believable that he could undermine anyone's own solid beliefs to sway them into thinking he was right. In my opinion, it was almost impossible for Michael to admit he was wrong about anything. I think he has a desperate need to be right, and look good all the time. This made him appear to be very insecure and arrogant. In retrospect, I don't recall that he was ever sincerely sorry about any disagreements we had, or anything he did wrong during the course of the relationship. He would rarely say, "I'm sorry," and say it only as a way to use it against me by some form of guilt-based manipulation. I know he couldn't possibly have ever meant any of it because he never really cared anything for me initially. Saying he was sorry was a ploy on my sympathies

to keep the current arrangement

going.

> *People who primarily focus on outward appearances and fitting in, are likely to be inwardly shallow, insecure, and unhappy. If they can't truly love themselves for who they are and who they are not, they cannot possibly love you.*

Chapter Six: Building A

"Normal" Relationship

During the entire course of my relationship with Michael, I worked full time for a publishing company from 6:30 AM to around 3:00 PM. In the early parts of the relationship, he was attentive, and very considerate. He is a very high energy person, and would frequently help out with the household tasks. Retrospectively, I now think that he actually justified not paying anything towards rent with the fact that he did laundry, dishes, and took out the trash.

He was an extremely early riser, and jogged and went to the gym very early in the morning. Battling an extra twenty pounds he said he needed to lose, his workouts were intense and frequent. From the gym, he usually went to Starbucks to relax and read the paper. He loved to go out to dinner, so we frequented some of the local restaurants several times a week. Particularly fond of Mexican food, he loved going to El Torrito restaurant in Oceanside. He would always pay for the meals out, and I would pay for the food we consumed at home. This seemed like a fair arrangement at the time, but in the long run became costly. It didn't connect with me during the relationship, but it seems like he wanted to impress people by throwing money around in public, and a restaurant was a good place to be seen out spending money. I paid all of the rent and utilities during the entire course of the relationship because he assured me that that he would put a large amount of money down on a house or condo for us, and put it in my name. (Claiming had some credit history issues that needed to be cleared up first, I saw no harm in that.) I thought the credit issues would be minor, and figured that they could be cleared up. That housing arrangement certainly sounded like a fair trade-off, and I openly agreed to it. As you can probably guess, that house or condo just never did seem to materialize. Had I not been so caught up in the overwhelming emotions of a new relationship, I think I would have surely questioned myself as to what type of person I was with. After all, what self-respecting man would let the woman pay for his housing needs, or anything else for that matter? I just didn't see it for what it was. I believed he really had a solid plan to get a house, and would stick to it. Unlucky for me, he had a completely different plan in mind than the one I thought we had!

We spent many hours during those (supposedly) romantic early times, just talking, laughing, or walking on the beach. I truly thought that we were in that bonding, and connecting stages of what I mistakenly perceived to be a real relationship. Michael has an innate understanding of the human psyche, and knows how to use his thoughts, mental energy, and words to get what he wants.

Many times he would claim that he doesn't have too many friends because most of the people he knows have too much negative energy, and that it's too much of a drain on him––he likes simplicity his life. I am still trying to determine how having

74

friends would be a mental drain, but lying, cheating, and stealing are not. You would think he'd be miserable with all that negative, deceitful energy within his own mind. Not this guy—I think he thrives on it! What is very clairvoyant to me now, is that he doesn't have many friends because he cheats all his friends out of money, then moves on to his next target. I guess he assumes friends are a dime a dozen, and there's always somebody out there who will want to hang around him for his humor.

Michael claimed to be a devout Catholic, and went to mass quite frequently at St. Patrick's Catholic church in Carlsbad, just down the street from me. He also attended the Monday night prayer group meetings and got to know many of the people in the group. Knowing that he was a Christian made me feel very comfortable at the time we met, mistakenly thinking that he shared many of the same values as I do.

In retrospect, I'm still not quite sure what he got out of going to church. He constantly spoke of Jesus to anyone who would listen, frequently quoting the Bible, just like someone with their finger on the pulse of true Christianity. I am not a foremost expert at different religions, but don't most of the

Christian churches preach the Ten Commandments as a cornerstone to Christianity? I know mine does. How does someone lie, steal, cheat people, manipulate them, and then claim to "walk with Jesus?" *How does that work?* He claimed that he frequently went to confession, so I guess in his mind that means whatever deed was done is now wiped out in the eyes of God. Based on results, he must have taken that to mean that it was OK to go out and do the same thing over again. *At what point will it really sink in with him—if ever?* The way I see it now, he's more like the anti-Christ nicely packaged into the body of a charming, and funny man, always ready to put a sword on your back. I once read that "going to church doesn't make you a Christian any more than standing in a garage makes you a car." A real Christian understands the true meaning of confession, and repenting. In Aramaic, (one of the early languages used during Jesus' time) the origin of the word repent means "turn and go in a different direction." I'm not Catholic, but I understand that the basic principles of confession are to ask for forgiveness, and then make changes in your life. I don't truly believe that confession is just a way of dropping off irresponsible actions into some imaginary dumping ground, then repeating the same behavior over and over again. I am not sure how Michael perceives confession, but his actions clearly do not reflect going in a different direction. It seems to me that this man is hiding behind the church to justify his fraudulent and irresponsible actions, and uses religion create a façade of non-existent righteousness for gaining people's trust.

During our many, lengthy conversations over the 21 months, we talked a lot about relationships, and everyday life issues. He openly revealed some details of his past relationships with women, omitting, of course, the part where he left owing them money. In each of his prior "long-term" relationships, he repeatedly blamed the woman for the termination of the relationship. One was too clingy, the other was too lazy, etc. etc. etc. Being an extremely attractive man, he claims that he doesn't really like to date the younger women who seem to openly make passes at him. "They're just too clingy, controlling, and insecure" he would tell me. (I'd be willing to bet that if any of those younger women were financially wealthy, there'd be an even larger trail of financial chaos and destruction because of him.)

Occasionally, Michael would invite one of my girlfriends out to lunch if I wasn't available. I thought nothing of it at the time, feeling secure in the relationship, since he always told me about it. I assumed that he was just bored, or wanted get to know my friends better so that it would make our relationship stronger. Being someone who likes to be the center of attention, he didn't much like being alone. He loved being in a position of having someone around him who would laugh with him. (Of course, you can probably guess what was really going on here, but I am not the jealous type, and never dreamed he was just using me all along for a free ride, while hitting on my friends.)

All in all, I thought at the time that we had a relationship that was normal, and was something that could develop into a deeper connection. He wasn't very fond of the term "girlfriend," so he always referred to me as his "friend" in conversations with others, or when introducing me to someone. I wasn't real thrilled being introduced as a friend, but got used to it, convincing myself that it was no big deal. However, since I was just being used, it's no wonder he didn't want to admit to being in a relationship with me. Of course, that one went right over my head too. It makes me wonder what he called the women in his past relationships. Or what about now? Does he introduce his current wife as his "friend" too? Or does he call her his "wife" because she's wealthy?

The one thing I did notice was that he seemed to have some real issues with intimacy, and didn't like hand-holding or kissing very much. In my mind, that was something I was willing to overlook as long as the rest of the relationship had strength. Silly me! There was no desire on his part to have *any* relationship with me at all—only with my money and credit cards. I was "overlooking" something that didn't exist—an imaginary flaw in an imaginary relationship.

I realize now how difficult that actually must have been for him. He was living a façade of love and caring for all those months— pretending to be interested in me and my life, pretending to have feelings that aren't there, and pretending that we are planning a future together. (After a while, I guess that would take it's toll on the best of con artists.) It was all just a dart game from the beginning; he had all the darts, and I was the bulls eye.

I know I should have picked up many times over, the reality that he really wasn't interested in me. Besides that "girlfriend" thing, all of his attention was given to developing *his* career interests. Not once did he ever ask me about my plans, goals, hopes, wishes or desires for my life. He even forgot my birthday in July, 6 months before our parting. I am sure that if he were asked a question today about what *my* goals are, or one thing that *I* wanted to accomplish in life, he wouldn't have a clue (and I can pretty much guarantee he wouldn't know when my birthday is). I think that we try and justify other people's behavior by convincing ourselves that it's OK to settle for less than what we really want. One truth I have learned through this experience is that we will always get in life what we settle for.

Intentions without action are merely excuses. A good con artist will gain your trust in any way they can, and promise you the world. They may even use a front of being religious to convince you they are righteous and trustworthy.

Chapter Seven: The Master Plan:

A Company is Born

Michael's self-deprecating wit and love of comedy made for some hilarious moments and many hours of gut-splitting laughter, especially during those first few months. Within the first three or four months of the relationship, I probed Michael as to why he didn't do stand-up comedy anywhere. He seemed to have a very special gift, and wasn't really happy if he couldn't make someone laugh.

(I believe that when you have a very strong desire to do something, it means that God is knocking on your door telling you to use the gift he gave you.) I praised Michael constantly for his talent, and continuously reminded him that he was given that gift to share. This seemed to affect Michael in a very profound way, and for a brief, fleeting period of time, I thought he could have possibly been on the road to a successful career in comedy.

After arriving home one day, he revealed to me that he had experienced a very intense emotional breakdown, and cried for hours. "I came out of the closet" he stated. He's always known in his heart that his sole purpose and existence was to be a comedian, and he could no longer suppress it. My relentless reminders struck a vein that had been buried within him his entire life, and he said that he now felt a great sense of freedom in acknowledging his innermost desire.

He became determined to follow through, and decided at that time to commit to this "divine" plan for his future. He desperately wanted to be famous, and thought that he could achieve that dream through performing stand-up comedy on stage. He idolized Sam Kinison and wanted to be his successor, using his crude but funny sexual skits and routines as a foundation for a new "star" to be born.

Wendy Quirk

"What is the next step?" we both pondered. I was happy to help Michael realize his dream of being a comedian, and supported him in every way possible. However, he was dealing with some personal issues that needed to be addressed before he could continue on. He had a terrible case of stage fright, and wanted to become more comfortable in front of a crowd.

He agreed to explore a couple of alternative healing processes that I recommended from personal experience, and that had been very beneficial for me in the past. My sister (Karmel Mangan of Spirit Whispers in Lawrence, Kansas) is an incredible new age healer and a Practitioner of

Energy Therapy, EMF, Reiki, Iridology, and Kinesiology. My chiropractor, Kimberly Rollheiser, of San Marcos, CA also does a wonderful healing process called Neuro-Emotional Technique, a process of clearing harmful emotions that are stored in the organs of the body. Michael agreed to work with both my sister and the chiropractor to become more comfortable performing his comedy routines. After several productive sessions with both healers, he then quit. He really started to make progress, but didn't continue. I guess he thought that he was just too good to make any changes, and hence tried to move forward to become a comedian, still battling many of the same psychological demons. From what I perceive, he couldn't handle looking at his own emotional issues, so he created a subconscious type of self-sabotage. That way, he wouldn't have to deal with anything internally and do the real healing work necessary.

We rented the old LaPaloma theater in Encinitas for him to rehearse his skits. He was really good on stage, as long as there was no audience. He ordered a remote microphone from a local music store, and used the store's loaner until the one he ordered came in, or that's what I was led to believe. (He actually ordered it in my name, and put down a deposit. He never picked up the new one, and kept the loaner without paying the balance. All this time, I thought he had picked up the new one, and didn't understand why I continued to be billed for it.)

He bought videos of Robin Williams, Sam Kineson, and other comedians, spending hours watching them, and studied their acts carefully. He also sporadically attended a local Toastmasters group meeting, to overcome his fear of public speaking and performing on stage. I went with him once to the Toastmasters meeting. He seemed to be somewhat comfortable with that group of people, and seemed to enjoy it, but didn't stay with it too long. I think he had expectations that he could take a few classes, or do a few speeches and instantly become a talented, successful entertainer. Anything that would involve a long-term commitment didn't seem to stay with Michael very long.

There is a local bar in Oceanside called Bub's Whiskey Dive that allowed Michael to use their stage for rehearsing. He made several attempts to perform on Saturday nights for the predominately Marine-based crowd, but something always went wrong. He couldn't quite pull together the comedy show routine, and the whole process became a complete wash. A severe case of stage fright, coupled with technical difficulties spelled repeated disaster, and after several attempts, he gave up.

For his next shot at fulfilling the fame and fortune dream, he went to LA and attended an acting class with Eric Morris, a very renown acting coach. After the first session, he decided not to continue on with the classes, claiming that he pretty much already knew everything they were already teaching him. *Hmmm*! For his skits, he bought props including toys and blow up dolls. He also joined a comedy group down in San Diego, but eventually quit going to the weekly meetings. He had difficulty with doing his comedy in front of the group, but got some good experience. It was short-lived, however. He thought he was better than anyone in the group, and decided that to continue going was also wasting his time.

During late summer and early fall of 1999, Michael was very intrigued by the idea of video-taping some of the Harley Davidson motorcycle events that are scheduled intermittently through out the country. He felt there would be a gold mine opportunity in selling the tapes to the riders. He did some market research and thought there would be a viable and profitable market for these tapes, based on the number of Harley riders there are in the world. There were only a handful of other similar tapes available for sale at the time, and he was convinced he could produce a better product. Becoming even more obsessed with being an entertainer, his plan was to incorporate his comedy performances into the videos by scheduling himself as the entertainment. Confident that a huge percentage of riders would want the tapes, he started to formulate a plan.

With absolute conviction, he began the process of becoming a producer. His first video endeavor was the

Annual September Heart Ride benefit, hosted by Harley's House of Harleys in Oceanside. He hired a camera crew to shoot the Harley riders as they charged their way up to a restaurant/lodge in Escondido for the Harley events and party that followed. Michael's comedy performance occurred during the peak of the lunch rush, and was pretty much considered to be just mildly entertaining. It wasn't really too bad, but he stated that the stage fright issue made him speak too fast and forget the sequence of the routine.

The final video of this whole event had some strong highlights, but never got produced. I really can't recall exactly why it was not produced, but he later had a dispute with the film company that produced that video, and a subsequent Flagship Productions/Flagship Entertainment video discussed in chapter seven. (It is my understanding that there were non-payment issues with the Heart Ride video as well as the next one.) Regardless of the issues with the Heart Ride video, Michael was ready to jump in full force and tackle the larger Harley larger events.

In order to achieve our dreams, we must be willing to take a look personal growth and development to remove the psychological blockages keeping us behind the walls of failure. Real change must come from within, so be careful of involvement with anyone who is afraid to grow. If they can't take a real look at themselves, they will never really see you either.

Chapter Eight: Momentum

From the fall of 1999 through summer of 2000, Michael spent his time making contacts, networking, and learning about the video industry. I let him set up a bank account in my name, and he opened a Post Office box in his. He openly admitted he had problems with his credit report, but took no action to clear it up, even knowing that I had form letters and guidelines to help accomplish that process. He convinced me that he really wanted to get it all cleaned up, but was just too busy to deal with it at the time. Many people have had some derogatory information on their credit history reports, and I didn't realize the magnitude of how bad his probably looked. Maybe he was embarrassed and didn't want me to see it, or maybe he didn't want me to know the extent of just how many people didn't get paid in his past so I wouldn't question what he was doing during the course of our relationship.

Another avenue he used for marketing his videos was to set up booths at various motorcycle events. He rented the tents and had banners made, along with t-shirts, flyers, and other marketing materials. At one particular event in the parking lot of Harley's house of Harleys in

Oceanside, he included a drawing for a free electric scooter he acquired at a discount through his contacts at the spa company. (He later confessed that when it was time to pull the winning name out of the box, he read off the name of one of his friends instead of the real winner, and kept the scooter.)

He met with camera crews, graphic artists, tape duplication companies, and shipping companies to get everything lined up for the next project: *The Motorcycle Summerfest 2000: Ensenada, Mexico*. A very close friend of Michael's named Bill Kennedy owns a motorcycle shop in Oceanside, and is very well known and respected in the motorcycle industry. Through Bill's network of associates in the business, he was able to provide Michael with some key contacts in the motorcycle event industry. Without him, Michael would not have been able to have inside access for filming the events. Bill was considered to be a "partner" of sorts, but did not enter into any financial negotiations or sign anything involving the company. Lucky him!

I provided support by creating the letters, contracts, advertising materials, and other documents necessary for a legitimate business. I clearly let Michael know that I did not want to be considered a business partner or be involved in his business in any capacity, but that I would help out in any way possible. By this time, we had been together over a year, and I still thought we were in a long term relationship. *That state of delusion and unreality caused me to make the most destructive decision I have made in my life.* Cash flow was an issue, and I made the huge mistake of letting Michael use my credit cards, borrow against the Harley in my name, use my car, and borrow money to help get the videos produced. Thinking we had a sure thing (and were a sure thing), my expectations about the business and the relationship were nothing but positive. I believed that I would get repaid as promised, and that we would continue on in a long-term relationship.

As the company took form, things began to get extremely hectic. I felt like I was working two full time jobs, and had no time to come up for air. Based on the projected number of video sales, I thought it would eventually be worth all the hard work. It looked like the company would be successful and profitable, and I never doubted for a minute that I would eventually be compensated for my work, for the excess mileage on my car, the money I loaned him, the credit card debt, and everything else he promised to pay. (In lieu of that, I ended up with a very large knife in my back. More like a dagger, actually)!

The Motorcycle Summerfest 2000: Ensenada, Mexico video was produced and sold through Amazon.com, and to the network of riders that attended. It was by no means profitable, but it had a nice outward appearance, and did make Flagship Productions/Flagship Entertainment look like an official company. The company started out as Flagship Productions, but somewhere along the line, Michael decided that Flagship Entertainment sounded more official, and would now be a separate division of the company.

The *Motorcycle Summerfest 2000: Ensenada, Mexico* video was mediocre—there were some nice action shots of the bikes blasting down the highway, and the majority of the video was shot in the Ensenada, Mexico bars and clubs. Michael was the emcee for the take-your-top-off contest in one of the Ensenada bars. He had a wonderful opportunity right then and there to use some of his talent and wit. He was certainly in his element for drawing on his repertoire of "dirty" jokes! Instead, however, he did a lot of screaming and yelling and didn't really go into some of his funny skits. I was surprised at this, since it was the perfect opportunity for him to perform with an audience and really get into some of his much-rehearsed routines. Actually, there is one very funny scene in the video, where Michael merges into a crowd of Mexican singers, lurking in the back row, then loudly sings off key. His real and natural humor was in full force, without trying to put on a performance, and it was funnier than anything he tried to do as the emcee.

One very decent thing that Michael did do during this entire process, was get permission to use the music of *34 Below*, a terrific and very popular alternative/rock band from

Carlsbad, CA. Incorporating their strong, upbeat sound with the video footage _greatly_ enhanced the first real video production of Flagship Productions/Flagship Entertainment. (You can check out the band's music and tour schedule at www.34below.com).

A few months later, I learned that Michael had more conflicts with the video-taping company for the *Ensenada Summerfest* video, and he accused them of over-billing him on production costs. I didn't realize at the time that this was a behavior pattern of Michael's. Clearly, he was just creating an excuse to cheat the video company out of their fee by stating that they were over-charging him for the production time. Michael claimed to me that he was being billed for time when the tape equipment was down and not working. I am sure that the billing was accurate and honest, and that Michael conned this person as well. Even if there was a discrepancy, the majority of the bill should have been paid.

(The filming company is on the list of creditors to be paid from the book sales. If you go to Amazon.com and search *Ensenada Summerfest 2000* in the VHS category, you can see valid information pertaining to their complaint about not being paid.) The sales were very slow for this video, but it was a completed product, and a

stepping stone to larger projects.

> *When a person doesn't accept financial responsibility in business transactions, it is a sure sign that they will be not be financially responsible in their personal life as well. Never loan your credit cards to anyone, unless you are married to them!*

Chapter Nine: Corporate Fraud

Still convinced that this endeavor could be profitable, Michael now had his eye on filming an even larger event, the *Love Ride 17* in November of 2000. He met with the owner of Glendale Harley, the founder of the Love Ride. That event is a fundraiser for Muscular Dystrophy, and has evolved into the largest one-day motorcycle event in the world. The Love Ride begins with a huge party in the streets of Glendale, CA right behind the Glendale Harley store. There they have live bands, merchandise booths, and concessions. Then the biker crowd follows a celebrity leader and heads up the highway. The final destination is Castaic Lake, where an even bigger party unfolds, complete with more celebrities, food, live music, motorcycle events, and contests.

Through Michael's aggressiveness and assertive qualities, a contractual agreement was created that would allow the Flagship film crews access to the events, concerts, and parties. In trade, the contract obligated Flagship Productions/ Flagship Entertainment to donate a portion of the distribution sales of the tape to the Love Ride Foundation.

I feel quite confident that Michael had no further contact with those people after the event. As of today, to my knowledge, no money was ever paid by Michael to the Love Ride Foundation. *He cheated a non-profit, fundraising organization, all the while bragging to anyone and everyone how much he supported their organization and how his videos would help them!*

Getting ready for this event was sheer chaos. I helped put together advertiser media kits, banners, flyers, mass mailings, and email promotions for the *Love Ride 17* Video.

In the spa cover business, Michael used a Developmentally Disabled Production Center in San Diego for his product assembly and shipping.

When promoting the Love Ride 17 video, he told people that he was still using that organization for the video distribution as well. I assumed that he would be using their services for shipping and packaging the Love Ride 17 videos. Since none of the videos were packaged or shipped from that organization, he must have thought that lie would make him look like someone special who was contributing and donating to a worthwhile cause. Instead, he had a mailing center do all of the packaging and mailing. Another false front of the con man!

The day of the Love Ride 17 event, Michael rented several vans, hotel rooms, and a helicopter crew (all on my credit cards), then hauled the teams of volunteers up to Glendale to work the video booths. The film crew got some really great shots of the street party from a boom crane, and the helicopter captured even more incredible footage of the thousands of Harley's that raced up the freeway to Castaic Lake for the all-day event party.

He set up booths at the Castaic Lake party, and sold the videos for $5 each. When the event was over, the total collected was about $6000 for 1200 videos. This was a far cry from the $40,000 - $50,000 he needed to keep the business going, so Michael relentlessly kept borrowing money from various sources, and continued using my credit cards. He made one $5000 lump sum payment on the credit cards, just enough to keep bring the balance down, keep me in his good graces, and continue to keep me positioned in a state of trust. According to his "calculations," the video would be distributed through multiple channels all over the world, and would make him plenty of money to pay everything and everyone back.

The *Love Ride 17* Video got produced, was very well received, and was actually quite good. It contains footage of such celebrity interviews as Robert Blake, Peter Fonda, Jay Leno, Branscomb Richmond, Dan

Haggerty, Pat Boone, and Willie Davidson, of Harley Davidson. The video also portrays some rare shots of Hell's Angels members doing wheelies and other stunts. Apparently, getting that stunt work on tape took some real coercion on Michael's part, but coercive he is! He said the Hell's Angels don't usually do that sort of thing.

The sounds of 34 Below, Creed, and several other bands provide the background music during the action, partying, and riding shots, making it very enjoyable to watch. I do not know what arrangements were made to obtain permission in using the other music on the video besides 34 Below, but I did not see any contractual agreements regarding the other bands. My guess would be that all other music was used without permission.

Michael actually shipped out the 1200 videos to those attendees who purchased the video at the *Love Ride 17* event. Things were really hopping now, and his ego was having a field day with his new self-made title—"Producer!" I set up the video for sale on Amazon.com for Michael, and he expected huge results.

Unfortunately, he probably sold a sum total of 50 tapes on Amazon.com, if that. He was never able to set up the other distributors or resellers he wanted, so that video was now the third successive financial loss for the company. The *Love Ride 17* video is still listed for sale on Amazon.com. (One of his large creditors had some *Love Ride 17* videos that were held as collateral, and that person is now selling them to try and recover some of their investment.) Still hanging onto the illusion of being a successful producer, Michael kept convincing himself that the business was progressing. He vowed to move forward once again, and film the next big event, The 2001 *Laughlin River Run*. Michael truly believed *The 2001 Laughlin River Run* would the catalyst that would culminate a string of failures into a success. He saw the next project as the turning point that would get him into the big leagues, and hopefully onto bigger stages, to perform comedy for bigger crowds.

Sometime during the course of the video business, Michael met with an very sharp older gentleman friend he knew from the spa business. After their meeting, this person loaned Michael somewhere around $30,000 for the video business. Evidently Michael did not sign anything, and had no legally binding agreement. How many people would trust that amount of money to a friend on a verbal agreement, no matter how close a friend they are? I suspect not many. *Michael barely knew this man, and still managed to finagle all that money without putting anything in writing or signing anything!!* This unsuspecting person also bought Michael a nice Movado watch. Now, I admit that I was somewhat naïve and completely fooled, but do you see just how good this guy really is? I definitely wasn't the only one gullible enough to fall into his trap.

I believe that the universe will not support anything for very long that is born out of deceit and non-truth. When you move from a point of honesty, God will open doors for you that you never dreamed possible. Anything based on a foundation of lies will eventually crumble.

Chapter Ten: The Relationship Shifts

After all of the chaos in November, I was looking forward to the holidays, and a break from the business. Michael went to Colorado to get a Colorado drivers license sometime around Thanksgiving, as I recall. He told me that he needed to keep his truck licenses valid, but it was all very confusing because he also had an Illinois and California license as well. He had a history of getting traffic tickets, and I am assuming that was a way to get out of paying them—keep shuffling the license from state to state until they catch up with you.

The stress of this business was starting to take it's toll on the relationship. Little things kept coming up that indicated Michael was probably unhappy with the relationship and really didn't care at all about it any more. As part of my morning routine before work, I would to listen to the Jeff and Jer Showgram on Star 100.7 in San Diego. They have one of the largest radio audiences in the country, and are extremely funny. Michael started complaining about how "stupid" they were, and would put on the jazz music station in the morning before I got up. I can only assume that he was jealous—they are funny and successful. He was funny, but was basically a fraud, and a nobody in the comedy world. Maybe it was just too painful for him to hear other people living their dreams, being funny, entertaining others successfully, and prospering in the process. Michael began to show other signs of unrest. He would disrespect my belongings, and once brought my new car back full of sawdust without so much as offering to clean it or pay for the cleaning. He scratched one of the outside mirrors on the car while backing out of the carport too quickly. He casually mentioned it to me with no care, concern, apology, or offer to fix it. (After the relationship ended, I realized just how much he really did disrespect me. He had left taking CD's, tools and other various items out of the apartment that I never saw again, even after I asked for them back later.)

December rolled in, and Michael seemed more and more withdrawn and discontent. He went to a holiday Harley party without inviting me, and basically all but shut me out of his social life. Still, he kept telling me that we were such "good friends" and our relationship was long term. By this time, I was confused, and started to see the cracks in the relationship, wondering why so many of the pieces of the puzzle didn't fit. *Why is he so unhappy when I have given him everything I possibly could? How can anything be missing? What more should I have done to make it work better?* By this time, he must have been totally burned out on trying to be something he never was from the beginning, a relationship partner. I think pretending to care about me for so long was taking it's toll on him, and was starting to make him miserable.

The holidays came, and he gave me a very nice designer purse for Christmas (conveniently charged on my

credit card which I later paid for).
"Gee honey, you shouldn't have!"

He left Christmas morning, and later admitted that he just hung out by himself, feeling lonely and unhappy with our relationship. As you can clearly guess, I was blamed for it not working any more. The best excuse he came up with was to blame me for not giving him enough attention. *I worked a full time job and spent the rest of my time helping him in his business and his comedy career plans, but I didn't give him enough attention?* Obviously there was a problem here, but at the time I was stupidly open to working it out, thinking there *was* something to work

129

out. He would look me in the eyes and tell me that I would be in his life for a "long, long time" and we were such great friends. Repeatedly he would declare that in order to be in a relationship, you have to be good friends or it won't work. Then, oddly, he would begin to talk about moving to Colorado. A master manipulator, he would change his tune just when I thought I had things figured out. The handwriting was already on the wall, and I didn't realize that he was probably planning his getaway to Colorado from creditors he knew he wouldn't get paid.

Michael told me repeatedly during the relationship how many great things he learned from me about life, relationships, children, parenting, and other things. Claiming he learned from me some really great things on parenting, I felt glad that at least something positive for him came out of our relationship. I have racked my brain for the past year trying to figure out what it was he really *did* learn. From where I stand, absolutely none of it was ever applied to his life, least of all to his parenting skills!

A very short time after Christmas, he was invited to a holiday party at the home of some people he knew from church and prayer group. In an unusual twist of fate, he invited me to go with him—a decision that would unknowingly change both of our lives. I am not sure to this day why, except for the fact that God must have planned it that way to helped me piece together the real truths about to unfold. We arrived at the party and were promptly greeted by the pleasant hosts, the Northrops. It was a very nice, quiet party in a lovely home in La Costa. During the course of the evening, I met Janet Northrop, a young woman in her 30's whose parents were the hosts. Later in the evening after the wonderful holiday dinner, she and I sat in one of the bedrooms and talked about various topics, including health and nutrition.

Michael joined our conversation later, after entertaining the rest of the crowd at the party in the living room. I was picking up a very strange feeling about something, but couldn't quite put my finger on it. In the course of the three-way conversation, Janet mentioned that she was taking a rowing class, down at the beach. We moved on to other topics, and eventually migrated back out to the hub of the party. The evening grew to a close, and a short time later we left and came home.

Within the next week or two, Michael mentioned to me that he decided he was going to take that rowing class. I may have been living in a cloud before, but his intentions were certainly obvious.

I can only assume that he wanted me to figure out that he was pursuing Janet because he didn't have the guts to come out and say it. A few days later, he pulled me aside and said he had something to tell me. "I kissed another girl" was his blunt admission and only comment. At first, I thought it was something that happened at a Harley meeting or out at a club, and that he was just blowing it off as nothing. I know that he is very social, has many acquaintances, and can be very flirtatious, so I would have no difficulty in believing or accepting that someone kissed him at one of the events or meetings. I didn't want to believe that he had been cheating on me behind my back, so I tried to give him the benefit of the doubt.

His real intention, however, was to try and throw me off scent, so he then insisted that he met the person he kissed in church. *He kissed someone in church?* That didn't make too much sense either. My suspicions were confirmed when I learned that it was Janet, and he had been seeing her without telling me since the party. I feel reasonably sure that he met her the same time as I did, and did not meet her in church.

I asked Michael what this meant and what his plans were, but he was evasive. Part of the time he would keep telling me that we will be together for a long time, and that "the kiss" was nothing. "I'm <u>done</u> with Janet" he declared adamantly and repeatedly. Literally in the *next sentence*, he claimed that we can't live together any more because it was suddenly against his religion. Being thrown emotionally a bit out of whack, I was totally confused, and tried to figure out exactly what was happening. The barrage of lies came so fast and furiously, that I stayed in a state of thorough confusion for days. One day he was going to be with Janet, and the next day she was out of his life. Each day the story would shift a bit, depending on what the motives were. *Then, several days later, the man actually had the audacity to tell me that he was going to be with Janet, but still wanted to keep living with me—-as friends!!*

In my opinion, if someone wants to end a relationship with me, then fine, so be it. I'm very independent, and bounce back quickly, even though I wasn't quite ready to let go. By this time, I was starting to clearly see the things I didn't want to admit to seeing before. Things like the disrespectful behavior towards me, the shady business dealings, lying, and other negative behavior. Yet, I still cried over this man! *Why is that no matter how bad a relationship can be, there is still something in us that makes us want to cling to it?* I knew it wasn't good for me to remain with this person, yet it was really painful to know that I had been cheated on behind my back and lied right to my face.

Oddly, I did feel somewhat relieved, in a weird way. The strain of his business had taken it's toll on my nerves, and I needed a break from it all. I looked forward to some quiet time to regroup and heal. Despite a slight sense of relief, it was still very emotionally draining and hurtful to see the hard reality that I had been used all along. It was especially difficult when I would go to bed at night, knowing that he still living under my roof while he was out with another woman. He would come back in the early hours of the morning and sleep on the couch after being with Janet. It a was a rude, inconsiderate, and hurtful thing to do to someone that had spent the last year and a half trying to help them in every way possible.

I asked Michael to quickly formulate a plan and move on. His only response was, "I'm sorry, I was swept off my feet." I had to repeatedly insist that he move out, because he was not taking any action that would indicate looking for, or finding another place to live. I needed time alone, and having the man still living under my roof after lying to me and cheating on me was just too much to take.

Each day thereafter for the next couple weeks, he would say that he needed just a little more time, and he would move out. Instead of trying to figure out how to get up on his own two feet and move somewhere by himself, I guess he was spending those days trying to weasel his way into someone else's house for another free place to live. After he finally left my place, the story from there gets a big foggy. I wasn't clear as to where he went, but he definitely revealed to me another hidden side of his psyche now brought to light during a conversation we had a short time later.

Here's where the story gets really interesting! He stated that there was an empty room at a friend's house, a gay dentist named Alex he knew through church. He admitted that he was somewhat attracted to Alex, and claimed that Alex wanted Michael as his partner, and invited Michael to move in with him. He also divulged that he was somewhat physically involved with Alex in a "love" relationship. To what extent, I can't be sure. The answers I got were wishy-washy, but the message was quite clear. Stunned, I couldn't believe what I was hearing! Evidently Michael was playing them both, manipulating both Janet and Alex, probably to see which would be more lucrative. I am quite sure that they both thought they were the only one Michael involved with in a relationship. What I find really unfortunate is that they supposedly all know each other from church, and I am sure that neither Janet nor Alex had any idea they formed the corners of his love triangle.

The disturbing thought of who else Michael may have been with, during and prior to our relationship, creeps into my mind occasionally, knowing what I now know. He made subtle innuendo gay jokes occasionally, but I always thought it was part of his comedy routine. The next time I saw him, Michael confessed that he decided he would definitely *pick* Janet, "because she's like a new car. She's never been married and has no children, so she can give me a lot of attention" were his exact words. At that moment, he omitted one very important factor—she's wealthy. *Very* wealthy. I'm guessing that once Michael discovered who Janet was, he decided it would be more lucrative to end up with her as opposed to Alex. You see, Michael then proudly informed me that Janet's grandfather was the founder of Northrop Grumman, one of the nation's leading corporations and the second-largest provider of information technology for the federal government. I was told by other sources that she was already somewhat well off, and also set to receive a sizeable inheritance (possibly at age 40, my sources say). There are conflicting stories as to the exact level of her financial worth, but in my opinion and given her lineage, that's why she was the "fortunate chosen one." A week or so later, Michael gave me the phone number to Janet's house in Oceanside and claimed that he was staying there now. I don't know if he ever stayed with Alex, or where he was staying during that time of confusion right after he left my place, but apparently Janet was decidedly the next target. Most likely, he told her some lie about me as to why he needed a place to live. I can't even imagine what story he concocted and told everyone to justify seeing her, while still living with me.

When you give everything of yourself in a relationship to make someone else's dreams come true, you compromise your own self-respect. If you don't respect yourself, the other person won't respect you either. Be true to yourself, and never compromise your integrity for anyone.

* "By putting other people's needs before your own, they will keep raising the bar to keep you loving them. No matter how hard you try, you can't make someone love you".

* Reverend Brian Anderson, First Church of Religious Science, Vista, CA

Chapter Eleven: Laughlin: A Sign of the Apocalypse

Spring brought all the gears shifting towards the *Laughlin River Run* event in late April 2001. I was thoroughly spent, burned out, and disgusted with the entire video business, not to mention Michael. Feeling like a shadow of my former self, I was still determined to try and hang in there until the *2001 Laughlin River Run* was over. There are approximately 50,000 plus riders at this event, and if even one tenth of them bought the video, I could recoup my losses and bring current the mounting credit card debt.

I let Michael continue to come over to use my computer with all of his files in it, and maintained the friendship in a positive way. Michael started to run out of money, and wasn't sure that he could pull off this event. I was not in a position to help any more, nor wouldn't even if I could have. I told him to give it up, take his losses and move on to what he really wants to do. It seemed like a mission of madness to keep going. He couldn't even figure out a way to get on stage at the Laughlin event to do some comedy, so why invest more money into the business? I think part of his persistence was the adrenaline rush for him—being the big producer, back stage press passes, telling everybody what to do and where to go, and having his name on the video. He still had everyone convinced that the Laughlin event would rake in thousands of dollars, so on a shoestring budget, he proceeded forward.

I knew he was out of money, but he was trying to pull off filming this event by the skin of his teeth. He kept insisting that he needed to do this event *just to get me paid back*. Yeah, right. I now believe in my heart, that even if that weekend would have generated a million dollars, he still wouldn't have paid anyone. I truly feel that he has it imbedded into his belief system that if you have a business you have to cheat people in order to be successful.

The morning of the 26th of April, I got up at 4:00 AM because Michael was scheduled to pick me up at 5:00 AM to head to Laughlin. He was almost an hour late, and I was furious. Instead of apologizing, he insisted that I had misunderstood the time. He had definitely indicated in our prior conversation that we would leave at 5:00 AM. *Does the man not accept responsibility for anything?* Why would someone lie about something so trivial? You would think it would be easier to just say, "oops, I messed up—-sorry." I don't know what it was, but he had a difficult time in admitting being wrong about *anything*. I think something in the make-up and personality of this person just couldn't accept anything other than always being right and looking good. The sad part, is that people always look a lot better when they are honest and admit their mistakes. Unfortunately, he just never grasped that concept.

Evidently, someone poor fool with money pulled through for him at the last minute, and the hotel rooms and other expenses were miraculously covered. In the van on the way, Michael made a comment to me that I thought was very unusual for him. He stated "You have no idea what I had to do to get this money." Usually, he would be bragging about how great of a businessman he was, and how quickly he could generate money whenever he needed it. To date, I have no idea who his last victim was, or how much he got from them.

We arrived in Laughlin that afternoon, and tried to coordinate a meeting with all of the other volunteers for the project. When it came time to check in to the hotel, I was informed that I no longer had my own room at the hotel, and had to share a room with Michael. I was very uncomfortable about this, since he evidently had intentions to cheat on his now girlfriend, or "friend," or whatever she was to him. I kept my distance and tried not be there whenever possible.

After checking in, we headed over to the offices of Dal-Con Promotions, the founders of the event. We were waiting for a particular man with whom Michael had previous contact. As I remember, Michael was supposed to sign papers, committing him to some type of payment for setting up the booths and selling the videos. I don't have any paperwork in my files or computer as to what was agreed on, but whatever payment Dal-Con were supposed to receive, I am sure they never got. Anyway, we waited for over 2 hours and the man with the contracts never showed up. We were standing in a nice, air-conditioned hotel room that they were using as the event offices.

While waiting, Michael quietly grabbed a handful of free passes to the events without asking anyone, and shoved them into my back pocket. Mortified, I didn't know what to say or do, and felt I couldn't very well create a scene with the people in the offices, so I walked out of the room. When confronting Michael as to why he did this, he thought it was no big deal, and couldn't figure out why I would be upset. Stealing is apparently a normal part of his life, so he must assume that everyone else thinks the same way.

Later Thursday evening after dinner, we went to see a very famous comedian—I'm pretty sure it was Howie Mandell. He performed stand-up at an outdoor theatre near the hotel. Michael smooth-talked the bouncer into letting us in on our press passes. The entertainment was really great, and the comedian put on a wonderful show. Interestingly, Michael seemed bothered, and wouldn't laugh much, saying the comedian wasn't very good. Then, abruptly, he insisted that we leave in the middle of the show. The only thing that makes sense to me is that it was probably too painful for Michael—I don't think he could handle seeing someone on stage living their dream, when he didn't have the guts or talent to do the same.

The video sales were dismally slow that Friday, the first day of the booth sales, but we prayed that things would pick up. From what I remember, we set up the booths at 3 (or possibly 4?) different event locations around Laughlin. The volunteers' rooms were paid for by Michael's last lender, so they didn't mind helping out with the booths. We rotated the staff so that everyone would get a break from the booths to party, participate in the contests, or just enjoy the events and concessions.

Friday night we had dinner at one of the hotel restaurants, and Michael announced to me that he and Janet were getting married in May, less than a month away. He was reluctant in telling me, probably (and incorrectly) thinking that I would get upset and be jealous. He had known her a sum total of less than 4 months. It certainly didn't surprise me, or bother me either for that matter. Quite frankly, I was really glad, knowing that there would be no reason for him to try and work his way back into my life for any reason.

Considering what I knew about Janet's family background, I would have expected nothing less from him. I couldn't help feel sorry for her, however, knowing what she was up against.

Michael seemed really proud of how intricately involved he was becoming in the Catholic church. He also stated during our dinner conversation, that he and Janet had been attending marriage and family planning classes for the last couple months, and he was becoming more and more involved in the church. From what I gathered, the classes were part of the process for couples to complete, in order to be married in the Catholic church. Just when I thought the entire situation couldn't get any more bizarre, another bomb dropped! Michael had been bragging to me about how good he doing was in the pre-marriage sex education classes required by the church. He elaborated on the various physiological details he had learned about reproduction, childbirth, and sex education. Then, he proudly announced to me that the Catholic church was planning on hiring him to travel around and give speeches on sex education at various Catholic churches. *Ok, now let me get this straight. The Catholic church is going to have an admittedly bisexual man give talks about sex education to*

its' members? Now there's a good one!
I don't think he just made that up,
so possibly he had conned even more
people than I imagined, convincing
even the church officials of his
"almighty righteousness!" After
hearing this, I don't feel quite so
bad about naïve I was. Like I
mentioned, he can be really, really
convincing.

By Saturday, things at the 2001
Laughlin River Run were in full
swing, bikers were everywhere, and
the video sales picked up enough to
shed a small glimmer of hope. While
working one of the booths, I noticed
while handing out the customer
receipts for the videos, that Michael

did not put his name or P.O. Box address on the receipts, and the only contact information that was on there was *my* email address. I asked Michael why he didn't put any of *his* information on the receipts. Of course, he blamed the printing company for making the mistake and forgetting his address, when it was a blatant set up in the beginning. *Right*! Oh, such Michael logic!

The filming crew was rotating around several different locations, depending on what event was going on. It was chaotic, and Michael was trying frantically to hold it together. He had to keep dodging the main camera man, because he was supposed to pay him and claimed he didn't have the money yet. At one point, Michael hid out in the hotel room feigning sickness.

There are a variety of different contests, competitions, and entertainment shows that go on during the *Laughlin River Run*. Part of the filming was supposed to be done on the nearby Indian Reservation, where some of the dare-devil biker stunts take place. I learned later from the angry Flagship crew, that the people running the events at the Reservation were so fed up with Michael's lies and manipulation that he was not allowed to go back to the reservation. If he did, there were a few hard core bikers there waiting there to "kick his ass!" He apparently told quite a few lies to his crew as well, because every time I saw someone from our group, they were as thoroughly disgusted with him as I was.

By Saturday night, we closed up the booths and I went back to the room. Michael came in and changed, announcing he had dinner plans with some other people from our group. Rudely, I was not invited. I never knew which rooms were assigned to the other members of the volunteer crew, so I wandered around for a while and had dinner alone in the hotel casino. I hit the streets for a little while, where thousands of bikers were milling about, or loudly racing down the main strip of Laughlin. Had it not been such a miserable weekend for me, I am sure it would have been a blast. Surrounded by thousands of men everywhere could be a rather appealing way for a single woman to spend a weekend in Laughlin!

Despite the excitement surrounding me, I was so thoroughly angry and fed up with the whole situation, I actually decided to leave. Immediately! It was about 8:00 PM on Saturday night, and it's a good thing I wasn't deathly sick or had a family emergency. *There was no way to leave Laughlin!* I checked buses, trains, planes, car rentals, and mildly considered hitch-hiking. Nothing!! I was stuck there, and there was no way out. Realizing the dismal results of the whole venture, I dreaded the ride home with Michael on Sunday even more. I finally succumbed, deciding it would beat walking home …but only by a *very* thin margin.

By Sunday, it was clear that this whole project was nothing short of a financial disaster. He probably sold a sum total of 100 videos at $5 each, and needed to sell at least 10,000. Michael blamed the catastrophe on the lack of teamwork and coordination of the volunteers, instead of the real truth. His insidious and malevolent behavior gave way to ultimate collapse. Through lies, fraud, and deceit his failure pattern once more repeated itself. He created chaos, started a fire, then rushed in to try and put out the fire so he can look good. This time, he created so much chaos that the fire got out of control, and burned us all.

The booths were scheduled to stay open until the late afternoon Sunday, but by around noon Michael seemed extremely frantic. He went to all the locations and hurriedly tore down the booths, throwing away the signs, and quickly packed up the van with the tables and booth poles he rented. In hiding from the unpaid event promoters, the camera man, and his crew, he needed to escape quickly.

The ride home was long and less than pleasant, but we had some pretty interesting conversations about his forthcoming marriage. I confronted him as to how he could possibly really love someone he had only known such a short while. Up until that day, he had never mentioned loving her, only how great her family background was. He paused before finally stating that he did love her, but it struck me as very phony and superficial, like he was pondering a business arrangement or trying to justify why he needed to love her.

When he finally dropped me off at my apartment, he left with all of the money that was collected, and all the forms containing the name and addresses of the customers who paid for the video.

Nothing works properly when ego gets in the way of common sense. We cannot solve our problems at the same level of consciousness that created the original problem. The height of insanity is to do the same thing over and over, and expect a different result.

Chapter Twelve: The Aftermath

For the duration of this book, some of the information about events that happened after our parting comes from reliable sources who were in close proximity to Michel, and people who shall remain unnamed in this book. I personally have reason to believe that everything told to me is true, but I can only state my opinions, based on what was disclosed to me. I will make clear reference as to which things Michael directly said to me, and to what other's divulged to me about his activities.

It was my understanding that Michael and Janet got married in one of the local Catholic Churches here in Carlsbad, California around the 3rd week of May, 2001. I am not Catholic, but it does make me ponder how a man who has been divorced twice can get married again in the Catholic church. I thought there were specific rules regarding divorces in the Catholic church, but I could be mistaken. If I'm right, I'd love to know how he pulled that one off!

I did not attempt to contact Michael for the next few weeks since he had just been married. Out of respect for his wife, I did not feel that it was appropriate that I call him so soon after the wedding. He did come by after he got back from his honeymoon in Hawaii to discuss the situation at hand. I found it interesting that there seemed to be plenty of money for weddings, trips to Hawaii, and everything else except paying his "friends" back. I heard that he told someone at Kennedy's Custom Cycle store that he would soon be paying all of his creditors. I think he wanted to spread that rumor around so that he could ward off the lynch mob until after he skipped town.

During our meeting, we discussed the financial situation, and I made it clear to Michael that he needed to help me with the credit card bills, even if it was only a couple hundred dollars a month. He *promised* I would get paid back, and would look me in the eyes and tell me what great friends we still were, and how much it meant to him to have me, my kids and his son involved in each other's lives. He emphasized the fact that I had become such a good friend to his older son, and that he valued that very much. *Typical. The man uses his own child to manipulate me into thinking he was telling the truth.* (But of course, why wouldn't he? He admitted to me that he used his son's Social Security number too.)

He adamantly confirmed that he would sign a written agreement stating that I was not responsible for any of his business transactions, that he would continue to make the loan payments on his Harley, and that he would pay all the credit card debt. Still clinging to his litany of promises, I drew up a 3 page agreement and scheduled a time for him to meet me to get it notarized. We decided to meet at the bank the following Saturday to get everything finalized. He came by and picked up the agreement, then left claiming that he had a job interview for a truck driving position and he needed to reschedule. My guess is that he took the written agreement with him and would forge my signature on it in the event of a court case. I think that was the same day that he tried to delete some files from my computer, then disappeared upstairs to my room. I can only assume that he was apparently looking for something. It seemed odd at the time, but the reason will unfold shortly.

He looked me in the eyes, *again*, and swore up and down that he told his wife <u>everything</u> about his debts and business failures. He also was emphatic that he cut up my credit cards. *Of course he did—I had already canceled them, and they were no good. I'm sure he'd still be using them otherwise!!*

As if everything prior wasn't bad enough, Michael then told another even more ridiculous lie—that he put a $5 bill in envelopes, taped the Laughlin customer name cards to the front of the envelope, and sent the customers their money back. Well it doesn't take a brain surgeon to figure out that when the customer doesn't receive something besides their little orange receipt, they will email me and complain. Granted he must think I'm really stupid to believe anything he ever told me, but how could he think he wouldn't get caught in *that* lie?

Months previously, I sold Michael my Geo Prism, and bought a Honda CRV. I took a loss on the Geo, but Michael had negotiated a really good deal on the Honda, so I decided to go ahead and get the Honda. After the Laughlin fiasco, he suddenly told me he sold the Geo to a salvage company. I really didn't care where the care was, but I asked him for the paperwork since the Geo was still registered in my name. Michael never changed the registration to his name, and I wanted to be sure I was no longer responsible for anything. "They didn't give me any" was the response he actually thought I would believe. It's a given that any company buying a vehicle would provide documentation. (Months later, the Geo was still registered in my name.) Another ridiculous lie and for what purpose? It seems like it's so compulsive for him that the significance of the lie doesn't matter, as long as he lies. I don't think he is actually capable of being truthful, even if he wanted to be.

He called one day soon after, to ask me if I had a problem with him taking the Harley to Colorado for a few months. His story this time was that his son planned to move there, and he was going to help him get set up in college. Sounding suspiciously like another lie, I told him that I was not comfortable with that until the credit cards and Harley were paid off. He began screaming and yelling at me like a little kid, "It's MY bike, and I can do whatever I want with it!!" I feel quite positive that he was running there to hide out from his creditors, dragging his new wife and oldest son with him. We re-scheduled the meeting to sign papers and he never showed. I finally had to accept the fact that he was not going to pull through with any money, and I was pretty much screwed! I knew things would change permanently from then on.

By late July, I had no response from my "friend" at all. The emails were starting to come in regarding the video, since those customers had no other source of contact. Knowing I had been set up, I told them to write him at his Post Office Box for a refund hoping the Post Office would be able to track him down. As of this writing in August of 2002 (over one year later) I am still getting emails about the video.

Despite the fact that I had still had not received any money for the credit card debt, Michael made the June and July payment on his Harley on time. Evidently he got someone in his family to make them for him, the motives being clear—pay it until he can sneak out of state with the bike. Sometime during the middle of August, I finally got Michael's address from his insurance company.

I went by the house in Oceanside where he and Janet were living, and saw a for rent sign in the yard. I knew this wasn't a good sign. *Was he splitting for Colorado soon?* It certainly looked like he was going somewhere, and Colorado was my logical conclusion, since he had talked about it so much. (He spent some of his childhood there, and still claimed to have a friend or two there as well. Actually one less friend now, as I will unveil later.)

Knowing I had to act fast, on August 28, 2001 I met with 2 officers from the Oceanside Police Department, and walked up the street with them to Janet's house. There he was, out in the driveway, loading a moving van. My intuition was right on target-he was definitely moving on somewhere. The police officers asked him if I was the owner of the Harley and showed him paperwork. He was cooperative, but only because I had two officers with me. I handed Michael a copy of the customers' emails about the videos and he tossed them aside, clearly unconcerned. I asked him where the Harley was, and my eyes followed his hand pointing to the moving van. *The jerk actually had the Harley (still registered and owned in MY name) loaded on the moving van, headed for Colorado!* The officers told him to take it off the truck, and they rolled it into the street to be towed. He had taken the mirrors and windshield off prior to loading it on the truck, and didn't give us those items, or the key. When the officer went back to the door to ask Michael if we could have the key, he claimed it was in his wife's purse. (That was not likely—he rode it everywhere.) Then, like some scolded little schoolboy, he went inside and called the police department, claiming that we were harassing him and had to get off of his property! *How mature is that!*

Obviously, I can only assume that Michael's plan was to forge my name (hence sneaking around in my room for a signature), quit making the payments, and get out of state with the bike. *Sorry Charlie! No can do.* That experience was decidedly the most embarrassing and humiliating position I have ever been in, but I was really glad I got that vehicle. I knew I wouldn't be able to make the $250/month payment on top of the credit card debt, and clearly *he* wouldn't pay anything when he got to Colorado either.

Within a matter of days, I had someone interested in buying the Harley. That party rode it to Bill Kennedy's Custom Cycle shop in Oceanside to get an estimate of what work needed to be done on it so I could sell it. I asked them for a written repair/estimate to be faxed to me. The potential buyer also asked for an estimate. Neither of us were able to get a quote in writing, but I was told by the mechanics that about $700 of work needed to be done, including the mirror and windshield replacement. We both thought the situation was a bit strange. Usually a written quote is standard procedure when doing estimates in the automotive business. The potential buyer and I finally agreed on a selling price and finalized the sale without a written estimate or further contact with Kennedy's Custom Cycle.

I recently heard from someone who was at a biker event in Julian, CA that Michael and Bill Kennedy had worked together at that fundraiser event. Clearly, despite all of the lies, and fraud on Michael's part, Bill had chosen to remain friends with Michael. I had unknowingly put Bill in a compromising situation by asking him to go against his friend to help me. It was not my intention to do that at all—I just wanted to give Bill's shop the business for any repairs that needed to be done. I didn't realize he intended to maintain the friendship with Michael, and I would have taken the bike to another shop had I realized that he would have been pressed to act on Michael's behalf in the situation. Regardless, I was able to sell the Harley, and pay of the loan—praise God!

I truly believe that good always comes to those who are honest. Somehow, it just always seems to work out OK when we come from a point of honesty, giving, and good intent. Divine truth was clearly present for me when I randomly show up to pick up the Harley at a fleeting moment in time when it was readily accessible, just hours before it could have been gone forever.

As the bible says, "The truth shall set you free." Lies perpetuate more lies until the truth becomes a mere shadow, tiptoeing through the far recesses of the mind. The universe always, and only, supports truth.

Chapter Thirteen: Doing my

Homework

Seeking clarity on my life and what I learned from my relationship with Michael, I slowly crawled out from behind that foggy cloud of manipulation and deceit I had been living in. I took the next few months off from thinking about my financial situation, Michael, videos, or anything else having to with the nightmare I'd just lived through.

The holidays came and went, and by the first of the year 2002, I was renewed. Feeling strong and confident, I formulating a plan of attack. By now, I had worked through most of the anger and resentment for being treated like a giant pin cushion for the back-stabbing swords thrown at me. I knew that I had to do something to try and recuperate my losses, but wasn't sure just how to implement a plan.

I spent the next few months putting together the exact amounts that Michael owed me, the interest on the credit cards, and other monies he borrowed. I contacted attorneys who indicated that I had a solid case, not only because of what he did to me, but what he did to everyone else as well. I researched out the people who worked on the project to find out who else got cheated out of their money, and created a list of creditors. I knew that once we got into a courtroom, I would have no problem proving my case, and would also have a string of other individuals ready to support my side as well.

Then one day I stumbled across an email from the camera company who filmed the Laughlin event. I contacted the owner/camera person who did the filming, and discovered that he actually *got paid* for doing the filming at Laughlin. *Why, I wondered?* The event was over, it bombed, and there was no clear reason why Michael would pay the cameraman, and not pay me or anyone else. He must have been paid after the event, because otherwise Michael wouldn't have been dodging him that entire filming weekend. He certainly wasn't a "friend" to Michael like I had been. He certainly hadn't paid his rent, funded most of the business, or put in hundreds of hours of free labor for Michael. He wasn't the one who got up in the early hours of the morning to go to the stage and hear Michael's comedy routines. So why did *he* get paid? There just didn't seem to be any logic to it all. There were so many other people that were much higher on the "pecking order" of creditors, with me first on the list.

I emailed the cameraman back to find out if Michael had possession of the film footage from the event, and if not, who did. I never got any response, and I took that to mean that Michael probably has it. *Did Michael actually want the footage shot at the event that badly? If so, for what purpose other than possibly feeding his ego a bit more?* Surely he wasn't going to actually try and produce those videos!

I still don't have any answers, but at that crucial moment of reality, then and there, I knew I would find a way to get my money back. Suddenly, taking the man to court seemed too easy. I knew I would win, but how would I ever get paid? He would just skip out again, but would it be worth a shot anyway?

Soon after, I was inspired with another idea. Several people who knew the entire story of what transpired with Michael, made me realize just how bizarre and incredible it really was. It hit me immediately! Publish the story, and tell the world what happened. Other people might want to hear about this so they can learn some real truths about con artists. Then and there, I decided that my story of what happened was going to be told, in print, for anyone in the entire world who wanted to read it. I wasn't quite sure how I was going to do that, but I just started writing away.

Where this will end up is in God's hands, but there has been a great sense of release in just writing it. When we see our mistakes in writing, it seems more real and true, and definitely makes the learning experience more effective. It became, for me, sort of a neutral and non-judgmental way to evaluate my situation and gain perspective on what I had experienced.

Sometime in the early spring, I put together a packet of papers containing the debt balance, all the receipts, and a 3 ½ page letter to Michael. I was feeling prepared and confident, and knew that I needed to take action. Even if I got no results, I needed to move forward and do this for my own self-esteem and integrity. I dropped the papers off at his wife's parents house, and his mother-in-law indicated that she would get it to Michael. (By the grace of God, I remembered how to get there, which is a minor miracle considering my normally frail sense of direction.)

I left all of the paperwork bound together in an open, Pendaflex file. I was hoping and praying that the Northrops would read the enclosed letter. I knew that I wouldn't get a dime from Michael, but wanted them to see what type of person their daughter had married. Maybe they saw some signs of trouble before, but I was hoping that perhaps I could save them or Janet some of the agony I went through. Even though it was decidedly none of my business, I still felt they should know their daughter married a con artist, if they didn't already know. (My sources heard there was no pre-nuptial agreement made between Michael and his wife, which was confirmed earlier to me by Michael himself). The Northrops are absolutely the nicest family you would ever want to meet, and I don't think they realize what they're up against. I would hate to see them be used, and lied to like I was. The letter below, along with photocopies of the receipts and other debt-related items, was given to his mother-in-law. I think the letter was a culmination of my frustration in trying to stay afloat financially, along with various incidents that I wanted made known to anyone else who may have read it.

Michael,

I find it very sad that you are incapable of being honest and having integrity, and that you value money more than people. I am happy for you and Janet, and contrary to what I am sure you are telling everyone as an excuse to not pay your debt to me and to blame me for everything wrong in your life, I am certainly not a "scorned woman." (A scorned woman would represent someone that would want the man <u>back</u> into her life). Why would I want someone back who only got into the relationship in the beginning to use me as a convenience until something better came along? (Like a nice girl from a wealthy family). Why would I want someone back who lied, manipulated, cheated on me behind my back, cheated on the woman you were supposed to be engaged to and then married, and stole money and other things from me? I made a very good living when you were living *here (for FREE), and if it wasn't for you, I would have almost no credit card debt —we both know that. I made enough money to <u>pay </u>for everything I needed. If you didn't owe me money for your business and personal debts, you would certainly never hear from me again, since you have made it very clear that what I perceived as a friendship and relationship was nothing but a con game from the beginning. I bent over backwards to help you out in your business, lending you my credit cards carte blanche and never questioned you about it, assuming that you placed some value on our relationship. I never worried about the fact that you* owed me money, or never paid anything towards rent and utilities. I stupidly trusted you to do the right thing. I thought I was in a long-term relationship, as you kept telling me, and didn't realize I was just being conned. What also really upsets me is that you destroyed something that I considered very precious to me, and that was my relationship with (your son). He's a fine young man, and I will truly miss seeing him. Because of your selfishness, lies, and deception, he obviously will not be able to be a part of my life any more.

The time has come for you to accept responsibility for what you *did—(for once in your life). You prey on unsuspecting, nice women and hide behind their name and their money for all your shady business transactions so that you don't have to accept any responsibility for anything. You manipulate them into signing documents for you and borrowing money for you in their name. You even use your own child's Social Security number as a way of avoiding responsibility. Then, even worse, you hide behind the church and use confession to justify your irresponsible actions, and have the audacity to call yourself a Christian. Since your too afraid to go after what you really want in* life, you keep using other people as a front, allowing them to support you financially, pretending all the while to care about them. That way, when there is one little bump in the road, you can bail on the relationship, blame the other person, and dump all the financial obligations on them while you suddenly disappear. I pray for you and Janet that you will not do the same thing to her that you did to me, and to all the women prior to me. Janet is a very nice person from a wonderful family, and doesn't deserve the damage you will do to her life, just because you have so many problems within yourself.

As for the Laughlin event, had you made a profit, it seems pretty obvious that you would have still kept all of the money, and had no intention of paying me back for your business and personal debts. (Speaking of personal debts, I noticed that you must have charged my Christmas present from Nordstrom's on my credit card. (I have never shopped at Nordstrom's but there is a $300 charge from there).

You planned all along to keep the money you collected from the video sales at the Laughlin booths, and not ship the video to all those customers who are still angrily emailing me as to why they have not received the video. (I have suggested that they contact you for a refund at your post office box address). Some of those people could possibly file fraud charges through the Post Office and report you. Since you probably gave a phony Social Security number to the Post Office when you opened the box, you are probably thinking that you can't get caught.

That explains why the orange receipts _you_ had printed and gave to the paying customers at Laughlin did _not_ have _your_ address or information on it—only _my_ email address. You set it up that way to nail me, and had every intention of stealing the money from the beginning. Why didn't you *just tell me that you spent the money from the few sales you had, instead of lying and saying you sent it back to those people who did buy the video? Since they have all now emailed me, did you really think you wouldn't get caught? (By the way, lawyers call that "intent to fraud.") Speaking of lies, why did you lie about the GEO? I know you didn't sell it to a salvage company. I legally sold the car to you (as a favor and at a <u>loss</u>) and I certainly don't care that you still have it, or who has it for that matter, so why lie about it?*

This big con game of yours also explains why you kept postponing the meetings to notarize our promissory agreements regarding the debt and the Harley. <u>Let me remind you that I loaned you my car, my credit cards, my money, and also borrowed money in my name against the Harley for your business, in complete trust, and you agreed to pay off the ENTIRE BALANCES after the Laughlin event, no matter what.</u> You also agreed to reimburse me for the excess mileage on my new vehicle as a result of your excess usage of the vehicle, as well as the other items listed on the attached chart.

You should be aware that in your haste to cheat everyone and skip town, you didn't quite cover all your tracks as well as you thought, and *this could cause serious complications and possible incrimination for you.*

I have retained legal council regarding restitution of this debt. You agreed to start paying this back 7 months ago, and have done nothing. I can only assume you mistakenly "took my silence as a form of weakness." (That is also one of Michael's favorite sayings). *It took me this long to gather information and all details of what happened, calculate the damages, thoroughly prepare my case, and obtain a good lawyer. To avoid very serious legal (and possibly criminal) repercussions for you, it would be in your best* interest to comply with getting this balance paid to me as soon as possible.

Based on the information about your history provided to my attorney by all parties involved as to the events that took place regarding Flagship Entertainment, (and how you conducted business), he has indicated that my case against you is extremely strong and that any forthcoming litigation would result in my favor. This will cost you attorney fees as well as the balance owed. Your credit card charges and all other debts to me that you agreed to pay are all verifiable by your signature on the receipts, as well as all of the *documentation in my files. (I have obtained duplicates of business receipts and documents you threw away). Of course, you know I have kept all the necessary documentation to validate my case.* (Michael used to complain all the time because I keep receipts).

Despite the fact that you were snooping around in my room after the Laughlin event bombed, most likely looking for papers containing my signature for forging purposes; and despite the fact that you tried to delete files from my computer, I still have everything I need to win a lawsuit against you, hands down.

The enclosed packet contains all debt verification, calculations, and

Mr. Integrity: 21 Months with a Catholic Con Man

debt deductions including the Harley sale. (It's too bad that you didn't take better care of it — then I probably could have gotten more money for it. It needed a lot of work, according to Kennedy's. Had you given me the mirrors, key, and windshield, it probably would have sold for more).

You should consider yourself fortunate that I did pick up the motorcycle from you. If you would have taken that bike out of state, it would have taken me about a day to find you, and right now you would probably be in jail for possession of a stolen vehicle. (Tempting as that was, I needed the money because the

209

payment was due, and couldn't wait another week. Obviously, since you had the Harley on the moving van already, you also intended to default on that loan as well). Were you planning to forge my name once you got to Colorado to get the registration out of my name and into yours? I put your motorcycle in my name (against my better judgement) as a <u>favor to you</u>, remember? —and the loan against your motorcycle was YOUR debt <u>for YOUR business</u>, remember?

Due to the magnitude of your irresponsible actions involved with Flagship Entertainment, you are still in <u>serious</u> trouble, and <u>you are sadly mistaken if you think that, just</u>

<u>because you skipped town, this will</u> <u>all go away</u>. If I have to hire a skip tracer to find you, that will get added on to this bill as well. Please don't insult my intelligence by thinking that you can hide out and not be found. I have all of the necessary information on you I need. Therefore, it would be in your best interest to get me paid <u>immediately</u>. As per my attorney's recommendation and calculations, the interest on this debt will keep accruing on the total debt at the rate of 15% per year, or 1.25% per month. Your next correspondence from me will be in the form of summons to appear in court. Upon receipt of the total balance

owed, all pending litigation involving all parties will be dropped, and I will never contact you again. Make check or cashier's check payable to me at the address below.

Wendy

I will probably have no way of ever knowing whether or not those nice people actually did read what was in that folder. I can only hold them in my prayers, because I know how difficult it must be for them to watch their daughter get caught up with someone like Michael. Even if they didn't read it, they must surely have to have some questions as to what was in it, and wonder why I would need to get important papers to

Michael.

> *Preparation brings self-confidence with no attachment to the outcome. Confidence is a reflection of who we are, and not what we accomplish. Jim Carrey once said, "It's not as important for me to hang on to what I have, as it is to hang on to who I am." Don't give up who you are for anything.*

Chapter Fourteen: An Update

I have some updated information in this chapter I obtained from people who have been in contact with Michael. In my opinion, all of this information is likely to be one-hundred per-cent true. The pieces all seem to fit, and my sources would have no reason to lie about anything they told me.

Firstly, for several months after I dropped off that folder, I was getting hang-up phone calls all during the day and night. That I can prove! I don't know what to say about that since it never happened before, but the timing was sure interesting.

Given some of the immature things Michael had done in the past, it wouldn't surprise me if he was calling and hanging up. During the early summer 2002, Michael was spotted back in town, staying out in Temecula. The exact same day I heard he was in town, a man called me asking for Michael. Up until that day, I had not gotten any calls for him in over a year. I will let you draw your own conclusions as to who called, but I think he put someone up to it, to find out what I would say. *But why?*

His wife became pregnant shortly after the marriage, and they just recently had a baby boy. I can't help but feel sorry for a child that will most likely grow up without a father, since I think Michael would follow his previous pattern of leaving a relationship after a couple of years. How sad that this man now has 4 children, 3 of with whom he apparently has little or no contact.

Earlier in the summer, I ran into someone I knew who mentioned seeing Michael frequently in church within the last few months, with his wife and baby. Knowing he was back in town, I did more investigating. It is amazing to me that the story continues to unfold with even more bizarre and unbelievable tales of woe.

From what was revealed to me, Michael started a trucking and hauling business while in Colorado. Since Michael had no money or assets when he got married, I can only assume any monies used to fund a business would have to have been from his wife. I am guessing he possibly used her savings or inheritance money. (She was working as dental hygienist or possibly dental assistant when we met her.) I also heard that Michael got a long-time friend from Colorado to invest in the trucking business as well. I'd bet my last dollar that there are no loans or obligations in Michael's name, and my sources also indicated that to be their opinions as well.

If I thought I had it bad, I <u>really</u> feel sorry for his wife now! Apparently he wiped out all their money, and ruined his wife's credit as well! I was told by my sources that his trucking business failed in Colorado and they moved back here…*after reportedly causing his wife to file bankruptcy, and supposedly wiping out about $250,000 of money that was probably part of her inheritance!* I am not sure about the bankrupt part because if he filed bankruptcy in his name, I probably should have been included as one of his creditors. (I'm not a lawyer, but

218

it would seem that all creditors would have to be included and notified.) I don't know what part the long-time friend played in the picture, but I heard that he was left in serious financial trouble. There were comments made about issues involving the business partner's signatures on certain documents that he claims he did not sign. I was also told that 2 of the trucks were brought back to California and dumped somewhere. Apparently the long-time friend was involved with the original purchase of the trucks and is trying to recover them. (Dumping the trucks is the same modus operandi Michael used with trucks from a previous trucking company he owned.) It looks like the swords were flying once more, and the con artist strikes again!

As of my latest report he, his wife, and baby supposedly are living in property owned by a wealthy relative of his wife's somewhere in Orange County, CA. Apparently he now has a truck-driving job for Chevron Gasoline Company.

Interestingly but certainly not surprising, I recently got a call from Michigan from someone looking for Michael. He was born in Michigan, and she was with the US Department of Defense asking for information on Michael's whereabouts. Hmmm!…sounds like real trouble to me when the federal government is looking for someone.

The problem with cheating and swindling people these days is that technology makes the world get really small, and mitigates hiding places. Where will he run now?

> *Always remember, no matter where you go, there you are. Who you really are will always catch up with you.*

Chapter Fifteen: A Profile of a Con Artist

This chapter gives a detailed description of my opinions and perceptions about this person with whom I was involved. Additionally, I am also giving you some other personality characteristics to be aware of, in hopes that you might be able to avoid involvement with someone like Michael.

I want you to get a very clear picture in your mind of this particular person, and how he thinks, acts, and lives. The characteristics and personality traits about Michael that I will describe in this chapter, are my opinions based on what I observed and experienced by being involved with this man. If you ever happen to have the misfortune of crossing paths with him, I want to be sure you will recognize him immediately, and have as much knowledge and warning as possible.

Be aware that he is really, really good at what he does—conning people. If you do meet him, believe nothing he says, watch your wallet, and run like the wind! I would almost guarantee that he will be on the lookout for another business opportunity, and possibly another partner to scam very soon. He doesn't like working for other people as an employee, and probably won't last long working for Chevron, or whatever company has currently employed him.

He is 42 years old, (an Aquarius), about 5' 10" with brown eyes, (usually wears glasses), brown hair, and weighing about 200-220 Lbs. He's attractive, and usually dresses in black Levi's and a black tee-shirt. If I had to chose someone he looks like as a comparison, I would have to say maybe a bit like Bill Murray. He's funny, *very* quick-witted, charming, attractive, and loves Harleys and big trucks. I'm told he drives a soon-to-be-repossessed white pick-up truck. He loves to tell jokes and will do anything to make you laugh. His sense of humor is crude, but creatively funny. He likes to talk to people and is very social, but don't be fooled—he probably wants something. (I don't think he really likes people, because he's too busy manipulating them to get to know anyone for who they are.) Michael is an early jogger and likes to work out early at the gym (possibly 24-Hour Fitness). He enjoys sitting at Starbucks reading the paper after his jog or workout. He occasionally attends St. Patrick's church in Carlsbad, CA. He had several different driver's licenses, and possibly uses different Social Security numbers. He is an extremely aggressive, fast driver, weaving in and out of traffic without signaling. He loves to dine out, and is sometimes rude, demanding, and condescending to the servers. He could possibly own another Harley by now, but I don't think so as of yet. He's likely to surface in more comedy classes in the LA area, or possibly at local Southern California open-mike sessions. He was recently spotted being an announcer at a motorcycle event in Julian, CA. He seems to prefer women, but would possibly become involved with a man as well. His relationships are usually short-lived, and he <u>always</u> blames their failure on the other person. In any type of financial transaction, he uses the expression "business is business." (Gospel, according to Michael.) He puts down people who are overweight, but admits to having excess weight to lose himself. He's sharp, alert, cunning, quick-thinking, and good with numbers. He never accepts responsibility for anything—it's *always* somebody else's fault. He never signs his name to anything legal. Obsessed about his looks, he loves that "Harley riding" image. He dislikes cops, the government, and any other organization that has to with rules or structure, calling them "society -based," or "bullshit."

227

Prejudiced, he makes racist comments occasionally. When trying to convince you how honest he is, he says "it's all good." Here's another famous line he uses — "it is what it is." He constantly talks about the Bible and Jesus, and how he "Walks with Jesus!" He lies incessantly, about anything, and steals whatever he can get away with taking. Another favorite saying is "you achieve(d) your objective."

In my opinion, he's emotionally unstable, disturbed, immature, somewhat dangerous, and admittedly bisexual. He is aggressive, and will openly claim *"I always get what I want."* He appears to be jealous of whatever takes the attention off of him. Oh, and after he learns of this book, he will definitely claim that everything in this book is "all bullshit" and that I am a "scorned" woman—-guaranteed!

Now allow me to put all of the pieces together to form a perfectly sculpted con artist. Following is my opinion based on my experiences. These are things I would question about someone else, were I interested in becoming involved with them. Certain aspects of their personality cause them to avoid accepting responsibility for anything. Instability in *any* area of their financial life is a huge red flag. Look for such things as repeated credit history issues, excessive traffic tickets, or disliking the rules and laws of our country. (Granted, most people at some time or another have had something negative on their credit history. However, I would be leery of someone who just doesn't care, or make any attempt to correct it.) Watch for comments about the government, Social Security numbers, cops, or anything representing structure and rules in society. This type of person will point the finger of blame on anyone else except themselves. Be suspicious of anyone who has more than one driver's license, and uses them. Someone who won't put their signature on a legally, or otherwise binding document has something to hide. If they have *ever* done anything to indicate they have altered their Social Security number, or used someone else's, beware! They may openly convince you they will sign any agreement, but when the time comes won't follow through. Based on my personal relationship experiences, here are some personality characteristics to be aware of, and watch for. Internal anger, sexual issues, sexual addiction, eating disorders, food addictions, aggressiveness, excessive profanity, rudeness, lack of respect for possessions, lack of respect for their children or ex-spouses, and basically all self-sabotaging or aggressive behavior.

In a business opportunity environment, they may try and con you by massively exaggerating the real profit potential, altering the books, and making false claims about assets. They usually have the innate ability to look you in the eye while lying to you. Be especially careful if they are really good at math and can mentally run numbers quickly, without putting things in writing. They like to move quickly into agreements to get your money.

If you suspect *anything at all* with someone else that seems shady, fly, fly away!! Run like the wind, sneak out the back, Jack, get the hell out...now! I guarantee you, it will only get worse.

> *When another person's values are inconsistent with our own, we must trust our instincts and internal feelings as to what is right for us. If we don't stand for something, we will fall for anything.*

Chapter Sixteen: Revelations

I am a firm believer in lessons, and know that nothing but good will come from my 21 month experience of living in a parallel universe of betrayal, darkness and deceit. It's amazing how differently I can look at the situation now, seeing so clearly what I so blatantly missed at the time. Why didn't I get out? — all the signs were there. Why couldn't I see them? I honestly don't have all of the answers, but I don't think my time with Michael was a fortuitous, random chapter in my life. I think those events in my life were supposed to culminate into the writing of this book, hopefully to benefit others in some way from the fruits of my labor.

In doing the writing, I was forced to dredge up the pain, take a good look what happened, and see how I reacted to it. In retrospect, I now realize those painful truths that previously blind-sighted me before. I gave up me to be loved by him—someone I now perceive to be incapable of loving himself or anyone else. I was so busy looking for some reasons why I should love this person, that I didn't want to see why I shouldn't. The most important thing I realized was that I didn't like the person I became in this man's presence. I compromised my soul, weakened my stand on integrity, and ignored the red flags waving boldly in my face.

There is no greater lesson than seeing the truth when you compromise your own self-worth, and try to live your life for someone else's dream. The bottom line is, you will always get in life what you settle for. I settled for someone with no integrity, honesty, or real compassion for others, just to be in a fun relationship. From our greatest vulnerability also comes our greatest strength, and I am now stronger, smarter, and more confident than I've ever been.

I trust that God will show me the good in my situation. Without my faith in God, I would currently be living my life in fear and hopelessness, harboring guilt for my blindness. I am trusting that the universe will continue to support me and my needs, and that God knows that everything I did in this relationship, I did out of caring, trust, and giving.

I believe that all of the real power of our lives is in our word. It can be our road to salvation, or the handcuffs that bind us to our own suffering and self-destruction. If our word can't be trusted, what else do we really have?

I gave up part of my individuality for this relationship. Our personality and individuality are our most precious possessions—that's who we are at the core of our soul. Our entire lives are a merely a process of life giving birth to itself while we are on the path that God has planned for us. I believe that every experience can be considered either a success, or a learning experience. There are no real failures in life—we learn lessons from every experience we have, no matter how badly we perceive it.

All our thoughts become our reality, and when our thoughts are based on truth, the experiences that reflect back to us will usually be positive. Jesus recognized this when he stated "It is done unto you even as you have believed." We always get what we believe, not what we want. Our problems in life come from the belief that we have limited possibilities and that we need others to get what we want, but those problems become the real stimulus to creativity. We can be inspired just when we give up on seeing the light at the end of the tunnel.

When life gives you lemons, there is always a batch of lemonade somewhere, just waiting to be made. I perceive Michael as someone who was a giant lemon in my life, and this book is my personal batch of lemonade. If

Wendy Quirk

we don't make the lemonade, all the

lessons become worthless.

"It *is better* to *take refuge in*
the *Lord, than* to *trust in man.*"
Psalms 118:8

Chapter Seventeen: Letter to a

Con Man

Dear Michael,

If you happen to hear about this book, most likely you'll rant and rave, calling me names, but it really doesn't matter. Since the book is dedicated to you, this letter is for me. It is a final good-bye and closure to a chapter in my life that gave me the greatest learning experience of all time. You have given me the opportunity of learning how to pull out of the worst of situations, overcome seemingly insurmountable obstacles, and find my true self. You rang the wake-up bell for me to stop settling for mediocrity in my relationships.

I'm sure there must be a reason that I came into your life, but that's not up to me to try and figure out. Maybe it's because so far, you've always managed to escape your con games without a scratch. Apparently, no one has stood up to you, or taken any action after you do your damage, and then quietly sneak away. What part of my letter stating there would be "serious repercussions" did you not understand? Did you think I was kidding? I did nothing to deserve the financial hell you put me through, and you know that as well as I do. So now, I must move forward on behalf of everyone who was cheated by you. If you feel the swords in your back now, it's only because they have come full circle from where you threw them.

You must be entertained at how gullible I was, believing your every lie. You probably snicker to yourself when you think of how you cheated me out of all that money, and stuck me with the bills, after letting me support you. Most likely, you laugh about the fact that you got away Scott free when you slithered off to Colorado, leaving me holding the bag. I guess you're also pretty proud of how you set me up to get the angry emails from the video customers. You probably don't worry too much about being sued, since the only thing you signed was your name while using my credit cards. I am sure it is entertaining for you to look at the mirrors and windshield you kept from the Harley. When you brush your teeth, you must be laughing at how you charged your dentist bill and new electric toothbrush to my account. How great it must be for you to wallow in the fact that you got away without ever getting me a birthday present, and made me pay for my own Christmas present. By now, you must not be overly concerned about how you cheated all your so-called friends, business associates, and organizations on the video projects, despite having the nerve to actually come back to this area. If nothing else, I'll give you credit for being the gutsiest con-artist around.

You had us all snowed, that's for sure. But guess what? *We* are *really* the lucky ones here. We can wake up in the morning, look ourselves in the mirror and know that our actions were based on helpfulness, teamwork, trust, and honesty. We are the ones who can go to sleep at night without wondering where to run and hide next, or if we will end up in jail. We are the ones who will never have to worry about the federal government looking for us. We are not living our lives teetering on the brink of self-destruction. We can live our lives in peace, truth, and integrity while maintaining our dignity—clearly concepts that are foreign to you. We're the ones that have the courage follow our dreams without needing someone else to pick up the tab for us along the way.

So what's next? Where will you run and who will support you after you deplete Janet's bank account, and destroy her life? Are you already on the prowl for your next victim, like some helpless child floundering in the ocean—jumping from lifeboat to lifeboat, afraid to swim on his own? Will yet another nice, unsuspecting, trusting woman (or man) bite the dust for you, a few more months down the road?

The way I see it, instead of following your dreams by way of discipline, integrity and hard work, you use and manipulate others, leaving them to pick up the pieces after you blow through their life like an F5 tornado of financial destruction. It seems to me like you also use people to fill you up emotionally when you don't have enough self-love to do it on your own, then berate them for not giving you enough attention. It will *never* be enough. The kingdom of God you seek is *within* you—real love and self-worth will never come from someone else, or somewhere outside yourself. The great spiritual leader Ernest Holmes once said, "Life is within outward, and never from without inward." Now's a good time for you to take a look inward. Is that possible?

Aside from the financial mess you left me with, the worst consequence for me is that you almost destroyed my friendship with your son. I understand that your "friendship" with me and *my* kids meant nothing to you all along, but you could have destroyed something I cherished. Some day, he'll realize the truth. As sure as the sun comes up tomorrow, the truth always floats to the top. You see, friendships are really important to me—people are important to me. Is that a difficult concept for you to grasp, since it's not about money?

I don't hate you at all, I just pity you and think it's pathetically sad the way you live your life—empty and hollow, dark, and devoid of the ability to really love anyone or anything, least of all yourself. Desperately trying to share your humor and make something of yourself, you seem to compromise that gift by trying to take the easy way out. Today, almost 3 years later, you're still just an emcee at a motorcycle event. What about that career as a comedian? It looks like you're still a scared "wanna-be" comedian, driving a truck, and most likely, still miserable.

I have never in my life met anyone with more charm, talent, wit, intelligence, energy, and determination that you have. Yet, I think you are the biggest waste of human potential that has ever walked this planet. Instead of living your life in truth, and relishing the gifts that God has given you, you stay in denial and waste your life away as a truck driver, apparently still trying to figure out how to cheat your way to success as an entertainer. Everyone wants to live on top of the mountain, but all the happiness and growth occurs while you're climbing it. Will you ever get it? Do you *really* think that you can be a successful, famous comedian and entertainer? Do you think that *anyone* in Hollywood or the entertainment industry would *ever* tolerate your lies, manipulation, and evil behavior, for even one minute?

Life gave me a lemon and I made a book out of it. So now the lemon's in your court. What will you do? Will you step up to the plate like a real man, apologize to the people you hurt, admit that you lied, cheated, and fraudulently gained our trust? Will you ever make any attempt to repay all those people? Be careful, someone might be watching now. Are you capable of feeling even one ounce of remorse for what you did? Or will you just stay in denial, and continue to blame everyone else for your business and personal failures? Who else will you blame now because *poor* Michael isn't happy, and won't do what it takes to be a famous comedian?

Do you really want to continue on this way, bouncing from one relationship to another, in the false hope that life will suddenly be perfect because of someone else? When you were with me, you suddenly became interested in health and nutrition and talked about it incessantly. Now you're with someone religious, and instantly everything is about religion, that you *never really practice*. Will you take your next unsuspecting partners identity like you take everything else? What would happen if you had your own identity, your own belief system? Based on your actions, it appears that you continue to hide behind other people instead of standing on your own two feet. Are you too afraid of the real person inside? The Bible that you think you so proudly quote says, "God helps those who help themselves." Will you ever help yourself? (And I don't mean to someone else's wallet!) Will you ever stand alone, and be all you could be, on your own? Is it that terrifying for you to look at who you really are, and possibly admit that some things need to change?

Your two "favorite" radio personalities Jeff and Jer at Star 100.7 frequently say to their listeners, "you need to go somewhere and get help." I always think of you when I hear that. Will you ever take a real look at yourself and get help to try and change your ways? This would be a good time—and was all that lying, game playing, and ego trip worth it?

True, you got away with hurting me, cheating me, and costing me a fortune, and have suffered no real consequences as of yet. But <u>know</u> this: I will move beyond where I am now, pay off the debts somehow, and be finished with all of this … forever. I can still live my life with integrity, and will honor my obligations. You, however, created a legacy of lies and fraud that will trail behind you and haunt you for years to come. You've become a small speck in history, your deplorable actions now solidified in print so anyone in the world can see the person you truly are. Are your own words coming back to haunt you now? Did you "mistake my silence as a form of weakness?"

You really should be thanking me—if this book is a success at any miniscule level, you might just get a small taste of the notoriety and attention that you so desperately seem to need.

Even with all the wit, humor, and talent you think you may possess, you will probably carry it with you to your grave, your jokes dying on your lips, and your epitaph reading, "Here *lies* Michael, the unknown comic." Touché.

If you intend to back-stab someone, make sure they don't work in publishing.

THE END

About the Author

Originally from Sterling, Illinois, Wendy Quirk has resided in California since 1970, and has worked in the marketing area of publishing for over twelve years. She is single and has two grown children. Her background in studying self-help, psychology, and metaphysical books played a major influence while writing *Mr. Integrity: 21 Months With A Catholic Con Man*. Wendy has also studied health topics for over twenty years, and is currently working on a second book about health and nutrition. While still an avid reader, she also loves movies, cooking, dancing, and skiing.